Sergeant York

Sergeant York

AN AMERICAN HERO

David D. Lee

THE UNIVERSITY PRESS OF KENTUCKY

Scholarly publisher for the Commonwealth,
serving Bellarmine University, Berea College, Centre
College of Kentucky, Eastern Kentucky University,
The Filson Historical Society, Georgetown College,
Kentucky Historical Society, Kentucky State University,
Morehead State University, Murray State University,
Northern Kentucky University, Transylvania University,
University of Kentucky, University of Louisville,
and Western Kentucky University.

Editorial and Sales Offices: The University Press of Kentucky
663 South Limestone Street, Lexington, Kentucky 40508–4008

06 05 04 03 02   5 4 3 2 1

Library of Congress Cataloging-in-Publication Data

Lee, David D., 1948-
  Sergeant York: an American hero.
  Bibliography: p.
  Includes index.
  1. York, Alvin Cullum, 1887-1964. 2. Soldiers—United
States—Biography. I. Title.
U53.Y67L44   1985   355'.0092'4 [B]   84-10465
ISBN 0-8131-1517-5
ISBN 0-8131-9028-2 (pbk.)

For Laura

Contents

Preface   ix

1. In the Wolf River Valley   1

2. In the Service of the Lord   14

3. The Shadow of Death   27

4. An American Hero   49

5. The Hero at Home   69

6. The Legend Makers   92

7. Last Years   116

   Notes   137

   A Note on Sources   153

   Index   157

Preface

In the last days of America's first war in Europe, Corporal Alvin C. York came marching out of the Argonne Forest with 132 German prisoners and a tale of individual daring unsurpassed in the nation's military annals. One of the least likely heroes in our history, York was initially a conscientious objector who was drafted only after his pleas for a deferment on religious grounds were rejected. However, his army superiors persuaded him that America was fighting God's battle in World War I, an argument that transformed the pacifist from the Tennessee mountains into a veritable soldier of the Lord. During the final Allied offensive of the war, York singlehandedly outshot an entire German machine gun battalion, killing twenty-five men in the process. His explanation that God had been with him during the fight meshed neatly with the popular attitude that American involvement in the war truly was a holy crusade, and he returned to the United States in the spring of 1919 amid a tumultuous public welcome and a flood of business offers from people eager to capitalize on the soldier's reputation. In spite of these lucrative opportunities, York decided to return to his native hamlet, where he spent the rest of his life working to bring schools and other public services to his mountain neighbors.

York's value as a symbol went far beyond his contribution as a citizen or soldier. He came to prominence at a time when the United States was reeling from the impact of the Industrial Revolution, a profound social and economic force that had changed a nation of agricultural villages into a great world power. In such uncertain times, York's pioneer-like skill with a rifle, homespun manner, and fundamentalist piety endeared him to millions of Americans as a kind of "contemporary ancestor" fresh from the backwoods of Appalachia. As such, he seemed to affirm that the traditional virtues of agrarian America still had meaning in the new era. Furthermore, York's victory over what was then the most deadly emblem of the machine age, the machine gun, represented for many the final supremacy of man over the instruments of destruction he had created. Thus, both York's personality and his achievement were balm for the anxieties that gripped American society in the troubled months after the Armistice.

York kept his hold on the affection of the American people for nearly half a century because he represented not what Americans were but what they wanted to think they were. He lived in one of the most rural parts of the country at a time when a majority of Americans lived in cities; he rejected riches at a time when the tenor of the nation was crassly commercial; he was pious at a time when secularism was on the rise. Consequently, for millions of Americans, York was the incarnation of their romanticized understanding of the nation's past when men and women supposedly lived plainer, sterner, and more virtuous lives. Ironically, while York endured as a symbol of an older America, he spent most of his adult life working to bring roads, schools, and industrial development to the mountains, the kinds of changes that were destroying the society he had come to represent.

Also, York caught within himself certain basic contradictions in the American character, most notably an ambiguous attitude toward violence. Although Americans insist they are a peace-loving people, violence has played a major role in shaping their history, and violent men from Jesse James to Theodore Roosevelt are heroic figures to many. The First World War highlighted these divergent feelings because, while the United States entered the conflict reluctantly, the nation fought with xenophobic zeal once Congress had declared war. As a conscientious objector turned successful soldier, York was a perfect reflection of America's reluctant but forceful involvement in European affairs. York resolved the conflict between his religious principles and his military commitment by deciding that to fight in a noble cause was to do the Lord's work, and his achievement on the battlefield apparently confirmed that America was indeed supporting a just cause in the remote and little-understood struggle in Europe.

I have had two objectives in mind in preparing this study. First of all, I have tried to penetrate the myth surrounding York to establish the facts of his life. What follows then is in part a biography that attempts to analyze the man and his achievements. Secondly, I am interested in the hero-making process itself; specifically, how heroes are chosen, the characteristics heroes exhibit, and the role institutions play in publicizing them. Closely related to this, of course, is the question of how heroes in turn manipulate the process that created them. In the case of Sergeant York, the press, Hollywood, and the army created a popular legend around York that presented him as the embodiment of certain values, but York in turn used the legend to advance his program of progress for his native Appalachian mountains once he had returned to civilian life. Although the wide acclaim he received greatly affected his life, his tenacious commitment to simple concerns enabled him to translate personal glory into a life of community service. Consequently, he claimed a special place in the hearts of his countrymen as a man whose life demonstrated the continuing vitality of the simple virtues of the common man.

Any attempt to study the life of Alvin York is plagued by some special problems. For one thing, York did very little of his own writing. Poorly educated and rather indifferent to popular acclaim, he was content to let friends express his point of view in prose more polished than his own. Three of the major sources for York's life—his "autobiography," his lectures, and his correspondence—are all products of other hands even though his name is affixed to each of them. Two men in particular served as York's scribes. Professional writer Thomas Skeyhill collaborated with the sergeant to produce York's autobiography in 1928, but York's personal secretary,

Arthur S. Bushing, played an even larger role in this regard. Throughout most of York's public life, Bushing prepared virtually all York's correspondence, and he probably wrote his lectures and speeches as well. Ironically, Skeyhill and Bushing tended to express York in very different ways. Skeyhill sought to convey the flavor of Appalachian speech by presenting the autobiography in dialect, while Bushing salted his work with words and phrases that were probably unfamiliar to York. Despite the disparity of style, however, they both worked so closely with York that it is still reasonable to assume they were accurately voicing York's sentiments.

Secondly, because York was asked to discuss the famous firefight literally until the end of his days, the evidence pertaining to the incident stretches over some forty years. For my purposes, however, I have concentrated on accounts prepared within a decade of the actual event. Apparently the story he gave orally to the army and the brief description he jotted in his personal diary are the only statements completely in York's own words. Both are very sketchy, but fortunately a *Saturday Evening Post* article done by George Pattullo in early 1919 provides added detail by quoting York extensively. In the mid-1920s, York cooperated with Bushing and Skeyhill in setting down fuller and clearer versions which are still in accord with the earlier documents. One of these became his standard platform lecture, a copy of which is held by the Tennessee State Library and Archives, and the other appears in the autobiography. Because no important discrepancies exist among these narratives, I have used them interchangeably in compiling my own summary of the incident.

I have incurred a good many debts since beginning this study several years ago. My colleague Joseph M. Boggs sparked my interest in Sergeant York and greatly influenced my understanding of his place in American life. Charles Bussey and Lowell Harrison also offered helpful suggestions, as did the anonymous scholars who reviewed the manuscript for the University Press of Kentucky. Brenda Kepley of the National Archives guided me to some rare and important York material not previously used by scholars. The staff of the Tennessee State Library and Archives led me through its unprocessed holdings on the York Institute. Nashville *Banner* reporter William Hance arranged for me to see the paper's clippings on York. Several members of the York family generously shared their memories with me, particularly Betsy and Howard Lowrey, Alvin York's daughter and son-in-law, who provided valuable assistance in numerous ways. I deeply appreciate their support. Grants from the Western Kentucky University Faculty Research Committee helped to defray the expenses I incurred. The *Southern Quarterly* permitted me to reprint portions of chapter 6, which appeared in the spring/summer, 1981 issue of that journal.

Not all the help I received was necessarily of a professional nature. Harper Katherine Lee arrived in this world just in time to supervise the final draft in her own enchanting way. My wife, Laura, deserves special mention. A direct and sensible woman, she skillfully coped with my irregular hours, preoccupied manner, and occasional absences over the lifetime of this project. I am grateful for the extra responsibilities she assumed so I would be able to write.

1. In the Wolf River Valley

Home for Alvin York was the Valley of the Three Forks of the Wolf River nestled in the Cumberland Mountains of Tennessee just a few miles from the Kentucky border. Here in Fentress County he lived virtually all his seventy-six years (1887-1964), in a stern and demanding land that his forebears had inhabited since the 1790s when his great-great-grandfather Conrad (Coonrod) Pile wandered into the valley and decided to stay. One of the "Long Hunters" who traipsed the mountains pioneering white settlement, Pile looms large in the folklore of the region. According to oral tradition, Pile built a cabin in the Wolf River valley and then went back to Virginia to secure a bride, a red-haired woman known as Pretty Mary. Her family opposed the match, followed the couple to the valley, and "kidnapped" Pretty Mary while Pile was out hunting. The determined Pile overtook the party and returned his wife to the Wolf River where they raised a large family and had many descendants, several of whom, including Alvin York, had red hair. In testimony to his spirited ancestry, York liked to joke that red-haired people such as he might end up in prison but never in an insane asylum.[1]

Usually prosperity bypassed the mountains to bless the flatter, more fertile meadows further west, but Conrad Pile thrived in the Wolf River valley. He became a successful Indian trader and merchant thanks to a crude yet unerring common sense. For example, he based credit on the supplicant's patches, reasoning that if they were on the front of his clothes the customer was a hard worker, but if they were on the back the man sat a great deal and was therefore not industrious. Prominent in the community, Pile numbered among his acquaintances an occasional hunter in the valley named Davy Crockett, and John Clemens, local politician, land speculator, and the father of humorist Mark Twain. Legend has it that Pile accumulated considerable wealth in the form of a keg full of gold coins which he kept hidden in his cabin. After his death in 1849, however, no keg was found, and the mystery of Pile's lost gold endures in Fentress County.[2]

The sound of gunfire echoed throughout the valley's history as the settlers killed to feed themselves and to destroy their enemies. Looking back on the early struggles with the Indians, York once remarked, "I calculate most every acre around those mountains was stained with human blood," but the Civil War fueled an even greater crescendo of killing in the Cumberlands. As former congressman and Fentress County historian Albert R. Hogue has written, "If there is such a thing as the fortunes of war, it certainly meant nothing to this county." On the border between unionist East Tennessee and secessionist Middle Tennessee, Fentress County became a kind of no-man's-land where bushwhackers and guerrillas wrote some of the most grisly chapters of the war. The fighting disrupted the local economy and plunged the Yorks, the Piles, and many other families into hard times that did not end with Lee's surrender.[3]

Not surprisingly, students of the region have found the Civil War to be the source of the largest single body of folklore in the area. "The people of this border country," one scholar has written, "were touched during the war years as no other people in the nation." Claiming token allegiance to one side or the other, marauding bands preyed endlessly on the civilian population, often with tragic consequences. The most notorious of leaders of these were Confederate raider Champ Ferguson and Union sympathizer Tinker Dave Beaty. A military court in Nashville convened in mid-1865 found Ferguson guilty of fifty-three killings, although he admitted the actual number was much higher. Beaty, a Fentress County native, was Ferguson's chief nemesis and himself responsible for dozens of killings during the conflict. After the war, some of Beaty's men known as the Wolf Gang continued to plunder the countryside until the state government intervened.[4]

Born barely twenty years after the war ended, York grew up in a society where the atrocities of Ferguson, Beaty, and others were still a vivid memory. The stories of those days were especially meaningful for York because the hatred spawned by the war had claimed the lives of both of his grandfathers. Uriah York joined the Union Army in Kentucky but soon fell ill and returned home to recuperate. Warned of the approach of Confederate troops, he fled through a winter storm to a remote cabin where he died a few days later of exposure. York's maternal grandfather, William Brooks of Michigan, came to the valley with the Union Army and stayed to marry Nancy Pile, granddaughter of Conrad. With his marriage, he became involved in the feuds of the Tennessee hills, particularly one between the Piles and the nearby Huffs, each family blaming the other for the death of relatives in the fighting. Brooks and Preston Huff, a member of the Wolf Gang, accidentally met at a grist mill one day shortly after the war and fell into a heated argument that climaxed in a shooting that left Huff dead. Brooks escaped to a Michigan lumber camp where his wife subsequently joined him. When the Huffs discovered their whereabouts by intercepting a letter, they succeeded in having Brooks extradited to Tennessee and lodged in the county jail at Jamestown. Before he could be tried, night riders abducted him and, as Alvin York told it, "tied him to the tail of a horse and galloped him through the streets of Jamestown and shot him to pieces." Typical of the folklore of the period wherein an innocent victim is horribly murdered, the story is the kind that people of York's generation would have heard often as they grew to maturity.[5]

Beyond the human toll it claimed, the Civil War also slowed the development of the mountains, and a half century after Appomattox, Fentress County was still remote, homogeneous, and poor. A fellow mountaineer claimed

York's native community of Pall Mall was "jest as far up in the Cumberland mountains as you can get without starting back in another direction." The railroad stopped ten miles short of Jamestown, the tiny county seat, and the York house was another forty miles by horseback over bad roads. Not until the eve of World War I did the first electric lights glimmer in a few Jamestown windows. Of the 7,776 people who lived in Fentress County in 1910, roughly 80 percent were descended from the original white settlers, while only ninety-eight blacks and thirty-eight people of foreign birth lived there. Because educational opportunities were limited, one man in five was illiterate, and one child in three did not attend school. Acutely aware of such problems, the editor of the *Fentress County Gazette* spoke for many when in 1916 he wrote wistfully of the day Fentress would "be in touch with the world and will be able to prove we have something worthwhile in this old county."[6]

Alvin York's youth was shaped by the difficult conditions of mountain life. Born in a one-room log cabin on December 13, 1887, he was the third of eleven children in a family that survived on hard work and firm discipline. William York squeezed a meager living out of seventy-five acres of farmland, did some blacksmithing, and kept order among his large brood with generous servings of what he called "hickory tea." Mary Brooks York did neighbors' laundry, often taking payment in old clothes which she then altered to fit her children. Because poverty forced responsibility on the children at an early age, Alvin was hoeing the cornfields before he was six, and even on days when his father excused him from that tedious chore, he was expected to help his mother with the housework.[7]

The boy's labor was rewarded with few luxuries. In the summer he wore a "linsey dress" and went barefoot, although for cold weather his father made ill-fitting pairs of stiff, brass-toed brogans, which Alvin softened in the heat of the fireplace before he wore them. Even then, the heavy leather "took the hide off my heels." When he was sixteen, his mother bought him his first pair of dress shoes. Extremely proud of his finery, he donned a white cotton shirt and his new shoes to wear to Sunday School, but his plans of impressing potential girl friends collapsed when a sudden rainstorm drenched his shirt and turned the path to a sticky red mud that pulled the heels off both shoes. Since he had no coat, Alvin arrived at the church soaked to the skin, his pockets bulging with the muddy heels.[8]

Guns were a major part of York's boyhood. William York was an avid hunter and quickly seized any chance to take his handmade muzzle-loader down from the rack. Since in the Valley of the Three Forks of the Wolf hunting was still more necessity than sport, Alvin began using weapons while he was yet very small. His earliest memories were of stalking snakes and lizards in the yard with a bow and arrow, and he could scarcely recall a time he did not own a gun. Because a poorly placed shot cost the family precious meat, his father demanded accuracy, and Alvin remembered that his father repeatedly "threatened to muss me up right smart if I failed to bring a squirrel down with the first shot or hit a turkey in the body instead of taking its head off." As he grew older, Alvin frequently went night hunting in the summer and was gone for days on end during the slow winter months.[9]

Organized religion and formal education played relatively minor roles in his upbringing. The mountain terrain interfered with the growth of churches, just as it impeded most other human efforts, leaving great chunks of the Cumberlands poorly served by the clergy. Like some two-thirds of his fellow mountaineers, William York did not belong to a church, and his wife rarely attended services, partly because of the demands of raising eleven children and partly because the minister preached only once a month several miles away. Consequently, young Alvin was an irregular churchgoer at best. His schooling was similarly limited. Almost fifty years earlier, his grandfather Uriah had returned from service in the Mexican War to start one of the first schools in the valley. Uriah's classes were in session for three months after the crops were "laid by," and his instructional materials consisted of the Bible, "a blue-backed speller," and a hickory rod. By the 1890s, the Fentress County curriculum had changed very little. Local classrooms, equipped with split logs that served as desks, were open just a few months a year and provided the mere rudiments of an education. Attending when his father could spare him, Alvin managed to reach only the third grade. Significantly, York, perhaps influenced by his grandfather's example, dedicated his adult life to bringing both religion and education to the mountains.[10]

An important period in York's life began in November 1911, when his father died of complications after being kicked by a mule. The oldest boy still at home, Alvin now assumed the enormous responsibility of supporting the rest of the family, and his life became an assortment of deprivations and disappointments. While the younger boys ran the farm, he operated his father's blacksmith shop, until a fire destroyed the equipment and forced him to hire out as a day laborer on railroad gangs and nearby farms. In spite of his efforts, he could never earn more than a few dollars at a time. His best job was driving steel with the construction crew building U.S. 127 through Fentress County, work that paid $1.60 for each back-breaking day.[11]

Seeking release from his frustrations, York "went all the gaits" as he "gambled, drank moonshine, and rough-housed," the traditional vices of the mountain men. Even his mother admitted, "Alvin was kind of a wild boy." A skillful stud poker player and card-flipper, his favorite hangouts were the bars dubbed "blind tigers" that straddled the Kentucky state line some seven miles to the north. There enterprising proprietors served their Kentucky customers in the Tennessee half of their establishments and their Tennessee customers in the Kentucky half. Thus a customer never violated the liquor laws of his own state and could therefore avoid a summons from his local grand jury. York and his cohorts staged spectacular moonshine drinking contests to see which man could consume the most and still stand, showdowns that York usually lost to his friend Everett Delk.[12]

Unfortunately, alcohol brought out the violent side of York's nature and often led him to confrontations involving fists or weapons. Standing over six feet tall and weighing 175 pounds, he had acquired the nickname "Big 'Un" and insisted he was never once beaten or knocked down by an opponent. Mary York said her son was slow to anger but, if trouble started, he would "go through with the job and there'd be a hurting." Although he always carried a knife and once tried to cut up a romantic rival at a church social, firearms remained his first love. Local tradition claimed that Frank and Jesse James were active in the Upper Cumberland after the Civil War, and the stories of their skill with weapons inspired York. The first book he ever read was an account of their exploits. Emulating his heroes, he began to practice with a six-shooter and quickly became effective with it. He could "crack a lizard's head" with a single shot using either hand and was occasionally seen galloping the mountain roads shifting the pistol from hand to hand as he blazed away at the spots on beech trees.[13]

A taste for alcohol and a fascination with firearms became a troublesome combination for York. Riding home one night, "drunk as a saloon fly," he saw six turkeys sitting on a fence some distance away and decided to test his sobriety by shooting at them. Six shots killed six turkeys, winning York a trip to court from their irate owner. On another drunken spree, he fell to arguing with Everett Delk about a white object floating in a creek. Delk insisted it was a pillow and York had no idea what it was; he shot it only to find it was a neighbor's goose. More ominously, he once sprayed bullets around the feet of a frightened enemy and ordered him out of the community.[14]

York funded his escapades with his rifle skills. Shooting matches had been a popular sport in Fentress County since pioneer days. One of York's favorites was the "pony purse" in which each man contributed a quarter or so and the man firing the most accurate shot won the money. The pots were occasionally as large as two hundred dollars and were supplemented by side bets that Delk often placed on his friend. In another type of contest, a turkey was tethered behind a log with only his head exposed, and the first man to take off the bird's bobbing head from forty yards away won the meat.

Competition was most intense when the men shot for "beeves." The contestants bought shots at a target and used the money to purchase a beef, which was then divided into five parts with the best shot getting the first choice. Most mountaineers were extremely accurate, so careful measurements were usually needed to determine the winner, although on one memorable occasion, Alvin York had all of the five best shots and drove the animal away on the hoof.[15]

York's rowdiness was tempered by the sense of duty he felt toward his mother and family. While he never allowed his escapades to interfere with his responsibilities, his mother was deeply concerned about both his physical and spiritual welfare. She often followed him to the front gate in tears begging him not to drink and was frequently unable to sleep until he was safely home at night. She especially dreaded the fate of his soul if he were killed in a brawl before he could be "saved" and told him she had begun to pray for his salvation. For his part, York began to fret about the impact of worry and sleeplessness on his mother's health.[16]

York was also influenced by his growing attachment to a neighbor girl named Gracie Williams, whose family owned 150 acres adjoining the York place. Although the Williamses were somewhat more prosperous than the Yorks and were able to send their daughter through eight grades in a one-room school, Gracie's upbringing was similar to Alvin York's. Both were parts of large families—Gracie was one of thirteen children—which thrived on hard work. "We all worked," she recalled years later; "We went to the field and worked just like men, like the men done." Thirteen years her senior, York first saw the neighbor girl a few days after she was born and later insisted that he had immediately picked her as his future bride. When she started to Sunday School, he told his teenage friends that the "girl in pigtails" would eventually be his wife.[17]

Because both York and "Miss Gracie" were protective of the details of their courtship, it is almost impossible to say when their relationship became serious, but the two saw each other often by 1914. Her path to school took her by the York

house, while Alvin's hunting forays and farm chores frequently brought him into his neighbor's fields. Still, the
romance had a difficult beginning because the Williamses
disapproved of York. Prominent in the community, Frank
Asbury Williams supplemented his farm income with service
as clerk of the circuit court. A deeply religious man who called
his whole family together for prayer every morning and evening, Williams saw York as a boisterous ne'er-do-well much
too old for his teenage daughter. One Williams kinsman
dismissed him as a "hell-raising, rip-snorting, no-account
boy." An even more important obstacle than her father was
Miss Gracie herself. She liked Alvin but refused to let him
call on her until he mended his ways, and she made her point
emphatic by joining a church, a gesture that, York said, "got
me to thinking." His romance would clearly be stymied if
he did not reform.[18]

More important than criticism from Miss Gracie or his
mother, however, was York's own mounting dissatisfaction
with his life-style. Part of this was his practical concern to
avoid problems. Drinking led to fighting, York had found, and
"was like to get me in a right smart of trouble." He had
managed to make restitution to the owner of the turkeys, and
the owner of the goose never found him out, but on one occasion he had been forced to leave the state to avoid a grand
jury investigation into various charges including firearms
violations. York realized that these brushes with the law
might one day have serious consequences. In addition, at age
twenty-seven, York was outgrowing his taste for rowdiness.
"I knowd [sic] deep down in my heart that it was'nt [sic]
worthwhile," he explained.[19]

Augmenting these feelings of discontent was York's growing religious faith. Since church services provided much of
the social life in the valley, York attended regularly after he
grew up, often leading the hymn singing with his strong tenor
voice. Now as pressure mounted from his mother and Gracie,
he walked restlessly through the mountains struggling to
come to terms with himself. In December 1914, evangelist
H.H. Russell arrived to conduct a mighty revival. His scalding

sermons added to York's inner turmoil and finally drove him
to the decision that only the church could give him the self-
control he sought:

> I began to pray for God to help me as a poor sinner to
> find some relief from my appetite for drink, for ciga-
> rettes, for tobacco, for card-playing, for swearing, for
> dancing, for all the things the world had that a man
> could not do and be a Christian. And I began asking par-
> don from God for the sins that I had committed and He
> for Christ's sake pardoned my sins and delivered me
> from all of the awful habits that I had . . . and my sins
> was pardoned first of January 1915.

In the eyes of the mountain faith, York had been "saved" by
a personal experience with Jesus Christ, but despite this, he
refused to join a church until several weeks later when, as
he wrote long afterward, "I had a longing in my heart for that
power that was delivered to Peter and the saints in the upper
room on the day of Pentecost and I sought it and got it . . . and
have it now. This I know!"[20]

York's congregation was the Church of Christ in Christian
Union, a small, fundamentalist sect, which imposed a strict
code of personal behavior on its members. Originating in
Ohio, the church broke away from the Methodists during the
turmoil of the Civil War period. Its founders blamed the war
on "unwarrantable meddling both North and South, and great
injustice and insane haste on the part of extreme leaders in
both sections." They believed Christians, including their
fellow Methodists, had exacerbated these problems through
political sermons and a commitment to denominationalism.
Instead, these dissidents called for a new church organization
minimizing the differences among people and avoiding participation in politics. At meetings in Columbus, Ohio, in 1863
and Terre Haute, Indiana, in 1864, delegates from a variety
of denominations formed a new church. Known variously as
the Christian Union, the Church of Christ, and the Church
of Christ in Christian Union, the new group established a

number of congregations throughout the Midwest and the Border South in the decades after the Civil War.[21]

Besides the Civil War, the holiness movement that swept the nation in the 1860s greatly influenced the fledgling church. Offended by what they considered the secularism and immorality of the period, many middle- and lower-class Christians felt that the churches were sliding into corruption along with the rest of society. The movement was especially strong among Methodists due to the "perfectionist" ideas of John Wesley. A controversial notion expressed in many forms, "perfectionism" held that a Christian received a "second blessing" called sanctification subsequent to his initial justification. A "justified" Christian was assured of salvation, but a "sanctified" Christian was freed of original sin as well. By the mid-nineteenth century, this concept was no longer a vital part of American Methodism, but the holiness movement seized it as its vehicle for spiritual rejuvenation. Disillusioned Methodists broke away to establish new churches committed to sanctification, an exodus that fed the growth of the Church of Christ in Christian Union, among others.[22]

The doctrines of the church reflected the stormy times in which it was born. Its basic principle, according to the Terre Haute general convention, was the "oneness of the Church of Christ." Calling also for "Christian union without controversy" and discouraging "political preaching," the church sought to minimize distinctions among Christians. As time passed, this theme became more pronounced because the new church proved especially appealing to powerless people from the lower end of the socioeconomic scale. These people without wealth or influence eagerly embraced a Christian fellowship that declared its indifference to such things.[23]

The Church of Christ in Christian Union also espoused the Bible as its "only rule of faith and practice." The church advanced no special creed but instead called on its parishioners to form their own interpretations of the Scriptures. New members were required only to confess Christ as their savior, accept the Bible as the revealed word of God, and pledge to study the book and follow its teachings as they understood those teachings. The organization of the church reflected this commitment to the primacy of the individual conscience. Virtually no denomination-wide administration existed, and local congregations were absolutely self-governing with full authority to select and ordain pastors. Even such basic sacraments as baptism were not established by the church but rather were performed in the manner each candidate felt was scriptural.[24]

Such a church attracted Alvin York for a number of reasons. Convinced he could not be a Christian without a great change in his personal life-style, York believed that the strict teachings of the fellowship would help him to achieve the self-discipline he sought. Like many others in his native region, York was suspicious of creeds and hierarchy, and he liked the idea of a local community of believers free to study and interpret the Scriptures as each one thought appropriate. This approach was in keeping with his own strong sense of individualism. Moreover, York was attracted to the church, at least subconsciously, because his social background was similar to that of most of its members. Poor and uneducated, York had no place in the ruling establishment in Fentress County. Quite naturally, he joined a church that generally attracted people of his class. Finally, York was drawn to the church by its pastor, Rosier Pile, another neighbor who had occasionally hired Alvin for farm work. Born in Fentress County, Pile had been educated at the University of Harriman and Maryville College before returning to farm and run a general store in Pall Mall. Ten years older than York and well known locally because of a stint as tax assessor, Pile became a kind of mentor to him in practical as well as spiritual matters.[25]

Alvin York characterized his forebears as "sharpshooters and pioneers and Old Testament folk," an analysis that does much to explain York himself. A man of strong, often contradictory impulses, he waged a constant battle for self-control. While his Old Testament heritage taught him a stern morality heavy with overtones of duty and obligation, he also relished the natural self-indulgence of youth and gloried in the pioneerlike freedom from institutional restraints that his remote home made possible. The inner struggle between these two aspects of his life came through most clearly in York's attitude toward violence. Always fascinated with firearms, proud of his marksmanship, and inclined to "roughhouse," he nevertheless knew enough about violence to dread its consequences.[26]

Religion, especially a fundamentalist faith with its stress on sin and redemption, had helped to shape York in the first place and now offered solace for his turmoil. For York, salvation represented an attempt to master himself as well as to begin a life of faith. In order to do this, York believed he could not simply modify his behavior but rather had to make a complete break with his past. His future religious testimony usually stressed that he had not "backslid" since the day his sins were pardoned, and he rarely talked specifically of the years before he was "saved" except to admit, "A feller does a heap of things he's ashamed of later, don't he?" Later in life, York wrote in longhand a brief account of his early years down to his 1915 conversion. Although it contains pleasant memories of family and childhood, the title of the piece, "The Other Life as it Was," indicates the alienation he felt from the impulses he battled so hard to contain.[27]

2. In the Service of the Lord

In the summer of 1914, about the time Alvin York was beginning to reassess his life, Europe exploded in conflict, but for
York, as for most Americans, the collapse of the peace meant
very little. Europe still seemed to be a distant place prone to
petty squabbling over obscure bits of territory bearing unpro-
nounceable names. Americans were confident that neither
the struggle nor its outcome would affect them and generally applauded President Woodrow Wilson's proclamation of
strict neutrality. Furthermore, the war seemed only to be the
latest evidence of the foolishness of European politics and the
wisdom of America's traditional policy of avoiding involvement overseas. To the people in Fentress County, Tennessee,
the war seemed especially far away. There was no immigrant
community whose strong ties to the belligerents might have
aroused passions, nor did much information about the fighting
reach the mountains. While the weekly *Fentress County
Gazette* carried brief accounts of the major war news on the
front page, it still devoted most of its space to farm prices and
the local social scene, and the state's large metropolitan
dailies, which provided better coverage, had only a limited
circulation in the area. As a result, Fentress Countians paid
even less attention than most Americans to the European
war.[1]

Alvin York fully shared the indifference of his countrymen
to World War I. Although he now anchored his life in his
religious faith, through 1915 and 1916 York still faced important problems much closer to home than the Western

Front. Most pressing were financial woes which left him unable to pay his taxes in either year and threatened the loss of the family farm at public auction. His plight was a major obstacle in his courtship of Gracie Williams, because her parents were not convinced he could provide for her; so, as Miss Gracie admitted, the two "courted on the sly a little while." York left notes for her in the rail fences that marked the property line and timed his hunting trips to coincide with her walks to the fields to bring in the cows. Finally York began escorting her the two miles to church with Mrs. Williams as their constant and skeptical companion. Since chores or bad weather frequently prevented them from meeting, they also exchanged a great many letters. In early 1917, the couple at last became engaged, a victory York explained by saying, "Her parents were against me but she was for me."[2]

Church work also took much of York's attention. His own background made him acutely aware of the limited availability of religious training in Fentress County, so he worked diligently to establish Sunday Schools for other congregations as well as his own. Always willing to accept church offices, by 1917 he was the second elder, the "singing" elder, of the Church of Christ in Christian Union and conducted the services when Pastor Pile was absent. In short, he embraced his new faith with the same zeal he had once devoted to carousing.[3]

The American declaration of war in April 1917 broke over the mountains with the suddenness of a spring storm. Leery of things foreign, bewildered and unmoved by the complex chain of events that had led up to the war, many mountaineers were suspicious of American involvement. As one contemporary student of the "Southern highlander" described it, "there was a general lack of understanding as to the causes of the war, the reason for our entrance into it, and particularly the operation of the draft." These feelings enhanced the mountaineers' ambivalent feeling about the federal government. Intensely patriotic people, they took immense pride in the government as a symbol of the nation but bitterly opposed any efforts by it to exercise control over their lives.

Thus, the government's plans to organize manpower, industry, and agriculture in order to maximize the war effort
sounded ominous to those fiercely individualistic people,
spawning such farfetched rumors as the notion that the
government planned to seize all canned goods in excess of
two dozen jars. The draft worked a special hardship on mountain boys, many of whom had never been more than a few
miles from home and had no experience in the kind of group
actions that modern war demanded. Thrown in with people
from different backgrounds, they were extremely homesick
and often returned late if at all from leave. The perplexity
many mountaineers felt is reflected in the story, perhaps
apocryphal, of the father who told his draftee son to shoot
Germans as if they were revenue agents.[4]

These same feelings also troubled Alvin York, who was
now torn between conflicting loyalties. Patriotism was a
strong part of his mountain heritage, and he was well aware
that his forebears had answered the call to arms. But
simultaneously other forces prodded him to stay out of the
fighting; most important was his church, which emphatically
condemned violence. Although the Church of Christ in Christian Union had no established doctrine of pacifism, the church
did have a history of resistance to warfare. Writing some years
after the Civil War, Elder J.V.B. Flack, a Methodist preacher
who helped to establish the new church, remembered the con-
flicts of the 1860s:

> We refused to vote in the [Methodist] conference for
> resolutions of war. We refused to pray for the success
> of war. We refused to bring politics into our pulpit. We
> refused to join the ranks that marched on the streets at
> war meetings. We refused to make certain war speeches.
> We refused to prefer charges against members of the
> church whom the fanatics accuse of being disloyal. We
> refused to preside at forced trials of good men who were
> tried for political opinions.

Moreover, war was a very real thing to people like York and
his neighbors who had faced a bloody civil war barely fifty

years before. The atrocities committed by Champ Ferguson and Tinker Dave Beaty were still vivid memories.[5]

This awareness only reinforced York's religious objection to fighting and left him with a difficult choice. Taught that both religion and patriotism were virtues, he was now troubled and uncertain because they seemed to indicate such opposite courses of action. The beginning of conscription only made his dilemma more acute because it raised the specter of the government forcing him to violate his religious beliefs by serving in the armed services. York described his state of mind in the clipped, terse sentences that often characterized his speech:

> I loved and trusted old Uncle Sam and I have always believed he did the right thing. But I was worried clean through. I did'nt want to go and kill. I believed in my bible. And hit distinctly said *"THOU SHALT NOT KILL."* And yet old Uncle Sam wanted me. And he said he wanted me most awfull bad. And I jest didnt know what to do. I worried and worried. I couldn't think of anything else. My thoughts just wouldn't stay a hitched.[6]

York's inner struggle intensified after he received his notice to register for the draft in June 1917. He prayed, studied the Bible, and wandered through the mountains night after night seeking to reconcile his Christian duty with the demands of his country. Pastor Pile, who ironically was charged with the task of registering people for the draft because of his position as postmaster, urged him to seek exemption as a conscientious objector based on his membership in the Church of Christ in Christian Union. In answer to the registration form's query, "Do you claim exemption from draft?" York scrawled, "Yes, Don't Want to Fight." Then, acting at Pile's behest, York filed four appeals, two with the Fentress County board and two with the Middle Tennessee board, but all four were rejected because the church had no creed except the Bible, a book subject to conflicting interpretations. The rejection staggered York, who believed his appeal was based on Holy

Writ and could not comprehend how a nation that claimed
to be Christian could deny his application; yet within three
weeks of his last refusal he was called to Jamestown for a
physical examination and a few weeks later, on November
15, was inducted into the army. Although he toyed briefly
with the idea of escaping to the mountains, he realized the
authorities would eventually come for him and thus submitted peacefully, if reluctantly, to induction.[7]

York's first weeks in the army were among the most miserable of his life. He had never been away from the mountains before and noted disconsolately that his training site,
Camp Gordon, Georgia, was "pretty flat country." He also
found himself "throwed in with a lot of Greeks and Italians"
and other kinds of people he had never encountered before.
The product of a very homogeneous area, York had had little
contact with people who were not white Anglo-Saxon Protestants and felt an enormous cultural gap between himself
and his fellow inductees, a feeling the "Greeks and Italians"
also shared toward this product of the mountain South.[8]

His discomfort was compounded by the army's way of doing things, a process that York, like millions of other new
soldiers, considered puzzling and ridiculous. For example, his
first morning at Camp Gordon was spent picking up cigarette
butts in the company area, an assignment York considered
odd for any soldier but especially for one who did not smoke.
Later, he was genuinely appalled by his first encounter with
an army rifle. Raised with guns, he always took good care of
them. The weapon the government issued him was full of dirt
and grease. Nevertheless, the recruit promptly set about clean-
ing and mastering the rifle—probably a 1917 Enfield—and
soon declared he and his weapon were "good friends." It was
an accurate rifle, York admitted, but he proudly insisted that
up to a hundred yards it was no more accurate than the
muzzle-loaders used back in Fentress County. Perhaps his
most alarming experience came when "them there Greeks
and Italians and even some of our own city boys" took those
rifles on the firing line where, unaccustomed to guns, they
"missed everything, everything except the sky." York himself
discovered that army targets were much larger than the

heads of turkeys and he "generally made a tolebly good score."[9]

At the root of York's unhappiness lay his lingering doubts about the morality of war, although he told his superiors nothing about his convictions until he was assigned to Company G, 328th Infantry, Eighty-second Division, a combat unit that seemed destined for front-line service. Then he went to see his company commander, Captain Edward Danforth, a Harvard-educated Georgian who quickly recognized the private's sincerity and took him to Major George Edward Buxton, the battalion commander and a devout New Englander who so impressed York that he later named a son for him. Buxton and York spent a long night discussing the Bible's teachings concerning war. The major began by quoting Christ's admonition, "He that hath no sword, let him sell his cloak and buy one" (Luke 22.36), and asked York if the Christ who drove the moneychangers from the temple would ignore German "war crimes" in Belgium. He pointed out that Jesus had told his followers, "For my kingdom is not of this world; but if my kingdom were of this world, then would my servants fight" (John 18.36). Buxton argued that the United States was an earthly government due the "things that are Caesar's" and therefore the Christian servants of that government should fight for its preservation. He ended by reading a long passage from Ezekiel (33.1-6) that suggested that the Lord expected his people to defend themselves.[10]

The conversation introduced many new ideas to York and left him more confused than ever. The strange camp setting with its endless activity unsettled him still more, so Buxton and Danforth gave him a ten-day pass to go home and collect his thoughts. He arrived in Pall Mall on March 21, 1918, having walked the last twelve miles over the mountains lugging his suitcase. Although Buxton had assured him of a noncombat assignment if he requested it, York's honesty forced him to analyze the major's ideas even though his mother, Pastor Pile, and the congregation all urged him to accept Buxton's offer. Finally he fled again to the mountains where he spent all of one day, that night, and part of the next day praying for divine guidance.[11]

That night on the mountain, York experienced, in effect, a second conversion, returning home convinced that God wanted him to fight and would preserve him unharmed in battle. As he put the issue to a disappointed fellow church member, "If some feller was to come along and bust into your house and mistreat your wife and murder your children maybe, you'd just stand for it? You wouldn't fight?" Just as his first conversion to religion had made him an active Christian, now York plunged into military life with tremendous zeal. When Pastor Pile invited him to come to the church to say good-bye to the congregation York pointedly refused, insisting that he would be home safely very soon. Throughout the rest of his military career his officers remarked on his calm, self-assured manner both in and out of combat. Highlighting York's new demeanor was an aggressiveness tinged with fatalism. To survive in battle he advised, "Get determined to get the other fellow before he gets you, keep on thinking about it and with that determination you'll come through." Set against this feeling was York's realization that fate often determined survival in war. A few months after he left Pall Mall, he wrote that whatever soldiers might do, shells would still burst in trenches, rain would still flood them, and lights would still silhouette doughboys as they went "over the top," so "what is the use of worrying if you cant alter things. Just ask God to help you; and accept them; and make the best of them by the help of God." With God, a man could make the best of his trials, but if he faced them alone, they would destroy his peace of mind.[12]

York's second conversion points up some significant aspects of his personality. First of all, he was something of a plunger who committed himself recklessly to whatever project won his loyalty. Perhaps out of an innate need for excitement, York seemed incapable of moderate or temperate methods. When he became a Christian, he had thrown himself into a severe, fundamentalist church and given his personal and material resources unstintingly. Now he experienced the same sort of emotional commitment to the war against Germany. Secondly, York had a taste for violence that he controlled only with difficulty. He had turned against his "hog wild" days, embraced the church, and insisted that he never "backslid" because he realized how easily he could fall back into his old ways. Thus, when patriotism offered him a legitimate release for his violent impulses, he grasped the opportunity with the enthusiasm of a religious warrior.

Unfortunately, Buxton's judicious handling of York was not typical of how most military authorities handled such dissenters in 1917 and 1918. To his credit, Buxton displayed an unusual degree of compassion in the matter. Local draft boards were very reluctant to honor pleas for conscientious objector status, and even those who received this exemption were sent to regular army training camps to await War Department instructions about alternative service. Although regulations called for these men to be treated with "kindly consideration," they were often harrassed by recruits bound for combat assignments. Of some twenty thousand men granted conscientious objector status by the selective service system, approximately sixteen thousand ultimately yielded to this pressure and decided to take up arms. Members of well-established pacifist churches usually encountered few problems from the camp officers, but men like York who belonged to more obscure denominations faced a board of inquiry whose members often derided claimants for their convictions. It was York's good fortune to be under the command of a superior who respected his sincerity and handled his case with integrity.[13]

The last step in York's coming to terms with the war came after he had returned to duty. On April 19, his unit moved to Camp Upton, New York, to prepare for immediate embarkation for France. With the war closer than ever, York began to realize that he had no clear concept of why it was being fought, so he once again visited Captain Danforth to ask for an explanation. Just as Buxton had stressed German "war crimes" in his earlier conversation with York, Danforth now portrayed the Germans as a barbaric people governed by reckless warlords bent on overrunning the world. For York, the explanation dovetailed nicely with the words of Jesus,

"Blessed are the peacemakers . . . ," and on May 1, he grimly sailed for France convinced that "we were to be peacemakers. . . . That was we-uns. We were to help make peace, the only way the Germans would understand."[14]

York and the other members of the Eighty-second Division were among the two hundred thirty thousand American soldiers who sailed for France during the month. Originally composed of recruits from Georgia, Alabama, and Tennessee, the division gradually came to include men from every state in the union. Former doughboy Laurence Stallings described it as a "medley of backwoodsmen and cottonpickers from Dixie alongside city boys reared in gangways between tenements and bartenders from neighboring saloons." In honor of its diversity, it was nicknamed the "All-American" division. Its commander was Major General William P. Burnham, a career soldier who had enlisted after failing to graduate from West Point and had risen steadily through the ranks. The emotions of many on board swung constantly between the fear of a submarine attack and the boredom inherent in two weeks on a troop transport, but York was too seasick to notice anything besides the pitching of the ship. By the time he docked in Liverpool he would have agreed with the anonymous doughboy who declared, "We'd had all the boat ride we wanted."[15]

Realizing that they were embarked on the adventure of a lifetime, thousands of World War I soldiers began to keep diaries for the only time in their lives. To these men, the time spent in uniform was a dramatic departure from normal events, and they turned to writing not only to record their experiences but also to rationalize and explain them. Arriving at his destination, York bought a "little black French notebook" and started a journal which he entitled "A History of the Places I Have Seen." As published in his autobiography in 1928, it contains almost daily entries, usually giving his location and perhaps a brief religious testimony. Although he recorded little about his activities, the diary is still an important source for York's overseas experiences, since throughout his life he remained very reluctant to talk about the combat he had seen. The diary is also significant in another sense because its mere existence underscores York's independence of mind and deep self-confidence. Captain Danforth forbade his men to keep diaries for fear they might be useful to the enemy if the men were captured, but York refused to relinquish the notebook when he was asked for it, explaining that he had not come to France to be captured. Thus he knowingly violated regulations and again asserted his faith that he would survive the ordeal ahead.[16]

The Eighty-second spent the summer of 1918 putting the final touches on its combat training before moving to the front. Almost immediately after it reached France, the outfit turned in its American rifles and drew British weapons instead. As Alvin York had realized, the 1917 Enfield was an excellent weapon, and he hated to lose a trusted piece of equipment he already considered a friend, but American rifles were in short supply. Since the army only had some six hundred thousand of them when the United States entered the war, the American military was forced to rely on its allies for rifles as well as other materiel. In addition, British soldiers schooled the green Americans in the realities of trench warfare. York had to take special pains with his lessons because his six-foot frame stretched above the parapet of trenches built for smaller men, making him an obvious target.[17]

In late June, the Eighty-second was at last rotated into its place on the Western Front. The Americans had drawn the southern part of the line stretching from the Argonne Forest southeast to the Vosges Mountains. The British held the northern edge of the line for geographic and logistical reasons while the French took the center, which covered Paris. Designated the Lorraine sector, the American trenches were connected directly to port cities by a good rail network, which meant that men and supplies did not have to move by way of the already overburdened rail system around Paris. The U.S. high command was pleased with this assignment because the German sector opposite them covered important coal and iron ore deposits as well as a major rail line. If the Americans could achieve a breakthrough, it could prove to be decisive.[18]

York and the Eighty-second first tasted combat along a stretch of the front known as the St. Mihiel salient. It jutted two hundred square miles deep into the Allied line, crossing the Meuse River halfway between Verdun in the north and Toul in the south. The Germans had established their position early in the war and had held it ever since, enabling them to honeycomb the area with an elaborate defensive system. An important part of their position was an east-west ridge outside the village of Montsec that provided them an excellent observation post for watching Allied activity. A French assault on the salient in 1915 had been a failure and since then the sector had been relatively quiet. The Allies used it for training troops and as a rest area for battle-weary units from more dangerous areas.[19]

On the night of June 26, York and his comrades moved into the line, as New England's Twenty-sixth Division, a National Guard unit, left. The motley Eighty-second quickly found that life at the front, even in a quiet sector, could be extremely unpleasant. The trenches were poorly engineered, making them both dangerous and uncomfortable. Drainage was a special problem: summer showers sometimes turned the trenches to narrow rivers of mud. The Germans added to the misery by their determination to test the mettle of their new opponents. Curious about the Yanks and eager to supplement their intelligence reports, they lobbed artillery rounds and gas shells at the newcomers while snipers picked off the careless. Occasionally they raided the American lines in an attempt to take prisoners. York was assigned to an automatic weapons squad and spent much of his duty time on patrol armed with the French Chauchat, an eighteen-shot automatic rifle he derisively called "sho-sho." To the Tennessee fox hunter, the Chauchat was everything a gun should not be—heavy, clumsy, loud, and inaccurate. All a doughboy could do with one was make a lot of noise and waste ammunition. York said that in a tight spot he would prefer an American sawed-off shotgun.[20]

The volatile mixture of faith and violence that so marked York's thinking stood out in bold relief through his weeks at the front. He read his Bible constantly and sometimes noted his thoughts in his otherwise terse diary. Simultaneously his opinions of the people he called "Greeks and Italians and New York Jews" were beginning to change. He had been struck by the way they weathered the ocean voyage that had so tormented him, and now he was especially impressed by their aggressive spirit in the trenches. He found that he sometimes had to scramble to keep up with his fellow squad members on patrol, and came to realize that his strange comrades were as "right-smart fighters as the American-borned boys." Significantly, York could see most ethnic groups only as stereotypes and could relate to them only as they proved themselves in battle. When they appear in his memoirs, they are usually seen chasing chickens and rabbits escaped from a captured German storehouse or brawling with each other in makeshift saloons. York was clearly fascinated by these men so different from himself, but they did not earn his respect until they had shown they were good soldiers.[21]

The Eighty-second did its first heavy fighting in the push to reduce the St. Mihiel salient in September 1918. American Expeditionary Force commander John J. Pershing had decided on this attack as early as June 1917, but it took over a year for the AEF to achieve the necessary size and combat readiness to make the operation feasible. The general and his staff decided to concentrate the attack on the south face of the salient where American troops were already familiar with the terrain. The order of battle placed the Eighty-second on the eastern shoulder of the line occupying a narrow segment near Pont-à-Mousson. Its mission was to pivot around the northwestern edge of the town and push the Germans out of its suburbs.[22]

The American assault was a poorly kept secret. German intelligence was very good all along the salient and was enhanced by spies behind Allied lines. When Eddie Rickenbacker, the celebrated American aviator, visited Paris in early September, he found that even taxi drivers knew of the impending attack and some knew what divisions were assigned to the operation. The recently promoted Corporal York found tangible evidence of these intelligence leaks within minutes of the Eighty-second's arrival in Pont-à-Mousson. The Eighty-second, as well as many other American units, had been to Pont-à-Mousson before because it had never been shelled in spite of its proximity to the front. Doughboy rumors said that the French and Germans had agreed not to bombard it, and that the Allies therefore used it as a rest area for troops. York first went there on August 16 and remembered it as "a kinder earthly paradise." Returning on September 1, however, York found a ghost town. Forewarned of the attack, the people had fled, leaving food still simmering on the stoves. Almost immediately, German shells began exploding overhead.[23]

At dawn on September 12, Company G, 328th Infantry went over the top. A squad leader in the successful assault on the small village of Norroy, York remembered the next four days as an agonized blur. The night the assault began, the Germans struck their exhausted attackers with mustard gas, forcing York to wear his "pesky" gas mask for hours. All about him he saw the physical and emotional destruction of his comrades. Some went berserk and tore off their masks to drink the deadly gas in gulps, while others fell from shell or machine gun fire. For York, the scene brought a test of faith that he never really resolved. Years later he said, "It was pretty heartbreaking for a simple mountain boy who believed in God to see all of those good Americans lying around." It was indicative of his values that York was most grieved by the fact that the dead would not go home again. Tortured in spirit even beyond the physical pain of the battlefield, York resolved his doubts like the true believer he was. While others cursed God or cursed the Germans, York, perhaps remembering the promise of the old hymn that "farther along we'll understand why," wrote in his diary, "The only thing to do was to pray and trust God."[24]

3. The Shadow of Death

A bloody morning's work in October 1918 lifted Alvin York from the obscurity of an infantry rifleman and recast him as an American legend. The story of those violent and chaotic hours has become the core of the York myth and has appeared in numerous books and articles since it first took published form in 1919. Unfortunately, most of these accounts simply borrow from each other without attempting any real scrutiny of the standard version of events, which York and the army provided in the months after the Armistice. In 1929, however, the German government finally reacted to publicity about York's exploit by compiling its own account of the firefight that made the Tennessean famous. Almost completely ignored in the United States, this document provides a unique perspective on an American hero and brings us closer to the truth about a spectacular moment in our military history.

Heroic though it may have been, York's work in the Argonne Forest was a small part of a massive undertaking. The American victory at St. Mihiel was followed by the Meuse-Argonne offensive, a big push designed to end the war before winter. The target of the drive was Sedan, a city heavy with memories of French humiliation by Germany less than fifty years earlier. Sedan was crucial to the Germans in 1918 because, as a major rail center, it would play a vital role if the German army were forced to retreat to the Rhine for a last-ditch stand. Its importance was compounded by the fact that the only other line of retreat lay over the Ardennes Mountains, terrain not easily passable in winter. If the Allies could take Sedan, the German army would be trapped.[1]

The drive for Sedan was part of a general attack Marshal Foch planned to launch from the North Sea to Verdun with the Americans assigned the most difficult sector, a stretch from the Argonne Forest in the west to the Meuse River in the east. As Pershing explained, "In my opinion . . . none of the [other] Allied troops had the morale or the aggressive spirit to overcome the difficulties to be met in that sector." The most serious problem the doughboys had to face was the Argonne Forest, an enemy bastion on their left flank. The terrain and the dense woods alone would have made the area hard to attack but, like St. Mihiel, the Germans had held the Argonne since the early days of the war and had made it into a formidable defensive position. The advancing Americans would first encounter barbed wire backed by machine gun units arranged so that if one nest were overrun, the attackers were immediately subject to flanking fire from other guns. Beyond the machine guns was an intermediate position that was fortified in depth and buttressed by artillery. Behind this rose the Giselher Stellung, the outermost of the three walls of the Hindenberg Line, each named for one of the witches of Richard Wagner's *Götterdämmerung*.[2]

Although the Meuse-Argonne offensive began on September 25, the Eighty-second Division was held in reserve and did not leave St. Mihiel until September 24, traveling first by railroad and then by bus. The bus ride was fascinating for York because the drivers were French-speaking Orientals he called "Chinamen." Years afterward, he told a friend, "I done never seen Chinaman [*sic*] before, and I jes couldn't keep my eyes off them." Alarm soon replaced fascination as the drivers tore recklessly along the narrow French roads. No one was hurt, but two vehicles turned over, convincing York that the "Chinamen" were more of a threat than the Germans. York's chauffeur was probably Vietnamese, as the French army was using colonials for such duties. The precarious ride ended at Varennes where the division bivouacked in the woods about four kilometers southwest of town.[3]

Kept out of the offensive for over a week, the Eighty-second drew a difficult assignment when it was finally sent into action. The left side of the American line was charged with clearing the Argonne and, as expected, the task proved to be very difficult. On October 2, the Seventy-seventh Division on the extreme left of the line was deep inside the forest when the first battalion of its 308th Infantry Regiment lost contact with neighboring units and became trapped behind German lines. Commanded by a New York lawyer, Major Charles Whittlesey, the unit was christened the "Lost Battalion" by the newspapers, although it was not really lost but was surrounded and cut off. Repeated attempts to break through to Whittlesey and his men were unsuccessful, and the "lost" unit's situation became steadily more desperate.[4]

The American high command now devised a daring plan to relieve the Lost Battalion and revive the stalled advance. Pershing and his staff decided to attack due west into the Argonne to seize the high ground along its northeast corner, a risky undertaking because the attackers would be subject to machine gun and artillery fire from three sides and their right flank would be open toward the enemy. Since the Eighty-second was the reserve unit on the left, its 164th Infantry Brigade under Brigadier General Julian R. Lindsay was selected for the assault, in spite of the serious problems the Eighty-second faced. First of all, it had changed commanders on October 4, just two days before the attack was ordered. Major General William Burnham was sent to Greece as U.S. military representative and replaced by Major General George Duncan, the former commander of the Seventy-seventh. Duncan had been ousted from the Seventy-seventh in August, partly for reasons of health and partly because headquarters staff inspectors were not happy with his handling of the division. Beside himself with rage, Duncan stormed at his medical examiners that he would resign and enlist as a private in any army that would have him. Finally his old friend from West Point days, John J. Pershing, stepped in and offered Duncan the Eighty-second.[5]

Unfortunately, the Eighty-second's troubles went beyond

questions of personnel. As Duncan observed, many military planners considered the assignment "a mission impossible of execution." For the attack to succeed, the 164th Infantry had to be moved into position to strike and the 157th Field Artillery had to be moved to support it, despite the fact that the roads around Varennes were already churned into mud and choked with traffic. Moreover, none of the division officers, least of all the newly appointed Duncan, had had any opportunity to reconnoiter the ground, nor were there any firm intelligence reports about probable enemy strength in the area. These would have been difficult problems for any unit, but the Eighty-second was still green, even by American standards. Most of its service had been in quiet sectors, and while it had been tested at St. Mihiel, it had played only a small role in the massive assault.[6]

On the afternoon of October 6, the 164th, which included Corporal York's 328th Infantry Regiment, started out through the mud to its "jumping-off" point. The Germans bombarded the road constantly, and by late afternoon a cold rain was soaking the troops as they dragged their equipment through the shellfire and the muck. Fall rains had flooded the Aire River, which lay between them and the Argonne, and they had to ford it in darkness without local guides. Somehow, both of the brigade's regiments, mercifully hidden by dense fog, were in position by dawn and the attack began.[7]

The 164th had been assigned two objectives. First of all, it was to take Hill 223 west of the town of Châtel-Chéhéry and from there drive on approximately three kilometers to the Decauville Railroad, a north-south supply line for the Germans in the Argonne Forest. The attack of October 7 secured its objective, with Hill 223 occupied by nightfall. The pressure from this advance forced the Germans surrounding the Lost Battalion to retreat, and the next afternoon, Whittlesey and his small band of survivors limped out of their positions to link up with the rest of the Seventy-seventh Division. For holding his position five days under intense enemy pressure, Whittlesey later received the Medal of Honor.[8]

Alvin York and the rest of the Second Battalion, 328th Infantry Regiment had spent October 7 crouched along the road west of Châtel-Chéhéry watching the First Battalion take Hill 223. About 3:00 the next morning the regimental commander summoned the company commanders of Second Battalion to a meeting and ordered them to attack from Hill 223 in the direction of the Decauville Railroad at 6:00 a.m. Within minutes Captain Edward Danforth was rousing the men of Company G. Corporal York put away his Bible and joined his buddies stumbling over the shell-pocked ground toward their attack line on the hill. A cold October drizzle chilled the air as German gas and artillery shells burst overhead. Since the First Battalion had not finished mopping up Hill 223 the darkness was occasionally pierced by sniper rounds and machine gun bursts. With his men still taking fire from the rear, Danforth barely reached his assigned position on time.[9]

Placed on the far left of the Second Battalion, Company G quickly realized it was facing trouble. An artillery barrage was to precede the advance, but the only outgoing shells the men saw came from a trench mortar being serviced by a solitary lieutenant. Like the other company commanders, Danforth arranged his men in two waves with two platoons in the first wave and two other platoons in support. York was a squad leader in the left support platoon led by Sergeant Harry M. Parsons. At 6:10 the Second Battalion started down Hill 223 and across a five hundred-yard valley toward the German position on the other side.[10]

In front of the advancing doughboys were the men of the Second Württemberg Landwehr Division composed of the 120th, 122d, and 125th Landwehr Infantry Regiments. Elements of the Forty-fifth Reserve Division held support positions. After the initial American advance on October 6, these units had withdrawn west of Châtel-Chéhéry to a line roughly centered on Hill 223; on October 7, the Germans retreated again when the 328th Infantry stormed their position. As the morning of October 8 broke, the Second Landwehr Division found its line pounded into a horseshoe wrapped around the narrow valley that led to the Decauville railroad.[11]

Tired and discouraged, the soldiers of both the Second

Landwehr and the Forty-fifth Reserve were nearing the end of their fighting effectiveness. According to American intelligence reports, the Second Landwehr had held positions in the Argonne Forest since 1914 and occasionally performed well, but by 1918 most of its young men had been sent to other units as replacements. Those left behind were older and war-weary. The entry in the division journal for October 8 says, "Our men have gradually lost every vestige of morale." Seriously understrength when the Argonne offensive began, the division was rated fourth class, the lowest ranking, by U.S. analysts. Although the Forty-fifth Reserve had once been considered a second-class division, it had "done a great deal of heavy fighting during 1918, without, however, ever particularly distinguishing itself." "Men deserted to the rear, to the enemy, and quite a few were punished for insubordination to officers, and some for refusing to fight," intelligence sources reported. "The morale of the whole division was very low." Writing a decade later, a company commander with the 212th Reserve Infantry Regiment confirmed the American assessment in virtually the same words: "The fighting value of the men in the trenches had sunk very low."[12]

These problems had been exacerbated by the constant pressure of the Allied offensive. Committed to the firing line since the attack had begun on September 26, the German soldiers outside Châtel-Chéhéry were suffering from mental and physical exhaustion brought on by the constant fighting and inclement weather. Some units were so spent that they did not even call for rations when the field kitchens appeared. To these tired men, the oncoming Americans were "strong and healthy looking individuals" who "were relieved every other day" and "had at their disposal all kinds of luxuries." For the average German soldier, the will to resist such fresh troops was steadily ebbing.[13]

Yet whatever morale problems the German army faced, its men were still tested combat veterans, and on October 8 the Second Landwehr and the Forty-fifth Reserve held a fine defensive position occupying high ground above the Americans on three sides. As the Second Battalion reached the center of the valley, the point of maximum exposure, the heights around the doughboys exploded in gunfire. Machine gun rounds and mortar shells poured into the valley from Champocher Ridge to the right, the high ground directly ahead, and a heavily wooded hill to the left. The advance seemed to melt away as the survivors threw themselves into shell holes, bobbing up occasionally to sprint ahead a few feet and dive again for cover. From his position in the rear, York saw the company executive officer, Lieutenant Stewart, go down with a wound, rise again, and then drop with a second, fatal wound.[14]

Realizing that the forward platoons were trapped, Sergeant Parsons decided to attack the machine guns firing on them from the wooded hill to the left. He ordered Sergeant Bernard Early to take the three squads on the left side, including York's, and move still further to the left to try to outflank the deadly guns. Depleted by casualties, the three squads totaled only sixteen men plus Early instead of the usual complement of twenty-four. Parsons watched them go with great apprehension. "It was an awful responsibility for a non-commissioned officer to order his men to go to what looked to be certain death," Parsons said later. "But I figured it had to be done. I figured they had a slight chance of getting the machine guns." The Americans slipped around the German flank and advanced roughly a mile and a half protected by the dense forest. Uncertain exactly where the enemy was, Early then deployed his squads in four ranks and began probing for the rear of the German position. Suddenly they blundered into two Germans wearing Red Cross arm bands. One man surrendered but the other fled to sound the alarm, with Early and his patrol after him.[15]

Ahead of Early's detail on that wooded hillside were elements of the 120th Landwehr Infantry, the 210th Reserve Infantry, and the Seventh Bavarian Sappers. In charge of the section of the line was First Lieutenant Vollmer, commander of the First Battalion of the 120th Infantry. Vollmer and his battalion had held their position in the Apremont Woods since the opening of the Meuse-Argonne drive, but early on October 7 the unit retreated amid heavy shelling. In the confusion,

Vollmer could not find the new position assigned to his unit, so he turned the battalion around and moved it forward again. As a consequence of this action, Vollmer lost contact with the troops on his left flank, leaving his men precariously isolated from the rest of the German line.[16]

Acutely aware of his plight, Vollmer was already working to remedy the situation the next morning when the Americans started down Hill 223. As the Americans plunged into the valley, Vollmer's men, in the words of one platoon leader, "greeted the enemy with a lively fire," a barrage that for the moment camouflaged the escalating uncertainty in the German ranks. Because he did not have enough men to form a solid line, Vollmer was establishing a series of machine gun nests at assorted important points when his task was abruptly interrupted by a tremendous uproar to the rear of his position. Vollmer rushed back to investigate, but before he discovered what was happening, he found several dozen men assigned to the 210th Reserve Infantry lounging at breakfast. Claiming they were exhausted from a night of marching, the men had dropped their belts and put down their weapons. Just as Vollmer reached the scene, several Americans broke out of the underbrush and began firing at the unsuspecting Germans.[17]

Early and his men were nearly as startled as Vollmer and the soldiers of the 210th. Although York believed his patrol had run into a headquarters detachment enjoying a leisurely breakfast, in reality Vollmer was desperately trying to persuade his reluctant troops to move up to the line. Taken completely by surprise, the Germans offered little resistance and promptly surrendered as the handful of Americans surrounded them. When one man continued to fire at York, the corporal killed him. Then, without warning, the clearing was swept by staccato bursts from machine guns hidden on the hill behind the camp. Huddled together in the center of the clearing, the Germans dropped safely to the ground, but nine Americans fell dead or wounded. Early and one corporal were hit while a second corporal was killed outright.[18]

Standing off to the left of the prisoners, York fell to the

Alvin York in uniform, 1919 *Brown Brothers*

WESTERN FRONT , 1918
ARGONNE OFFENSIVE

Sedan

Chiers River

FRANCE-BELGIUM BORDER

BELGIUM

Arlon

Virton

Montmedy

Chiers River

0   10
Miles

FRANCE

Stenay

Loison River

Longuyon

area of EXPLOIT
map

GISELHER STELLUNG

Dun-sur-Meuse

N

Attack of
328th Inf

Chatel-
Chéhéry

Montfaucon

Consenvoye

Varennes

Malancourt

Etain

ARGONNE FOREST

Verdun

St. Menehould

Clermont

Aire River

Meuse River

Montsec

St. Mihiel

Bryan Kinkel

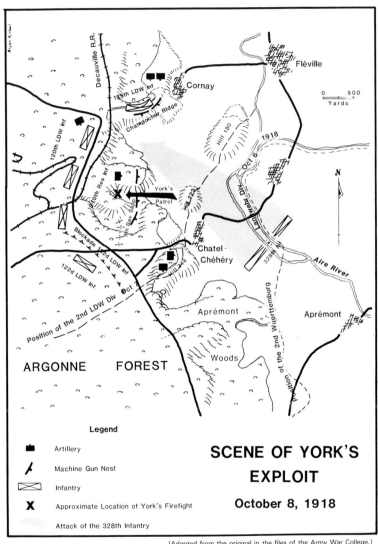

Legend

◼ Artillery

⌐ Machine Gun Nest

⬚ Infantry

X Approximate Location of York's Firefight

Attack of the 328th Infantry

SCENE OF YORK'S EXPLOIT

October 8, 1918

(Adapted from the original in the files of the Army War College.)

Above, York at the scene of the firefight. This photograph appeared with George Pattullo's article in the *Saturday Evening Post*. *National Archives.* Below, York at a press conference aboard the SS *Ohioan* on his return from France, 1919. *Bettmann Archive*

Above, Gary Cooper and York, 1941; right, York viewing a scene from the movie *Museum of Modern Art/Film Stills Archive*

Above, supper
table scene from
the movie
*Museum of Mod-
ern Art/Film
Stills Archive*

Left, York with his
mother in front of
their home, 1919
Bettmann Archive

York Agricultural Institute, 1931 *Nashville Tennessean*

The York home, 1939 *Nashville Tennessean*

Above, York with Pastor Pile, 1942; below, York with his brothers Rob and Sam and his youngest son, Thomas Jefferson York, 1942 *Nashville Tennessean*

ground as the firing started. Bullets sent an old canteen close to his hand dancing across the ground and a nearby shrapnel helmet was "all sorter sieved, jes like the top of a pepper box." With his buddies pinned down or seeking cover, York, lying between the prisoners and the gunners some thirty yards up the hillside in front of him, went on the offensive. He was so close to the gunners that they had to depress the angle of their fire in order to hit him, but he also was very close to the prisoners, so the gunners had to look before firing. The veteran of many a Fentress County turkey shoot rolled over to a sitting position and waited for heads to bob up. Keeping a .45 Colt automatic dangling from a finger of his right hand, York "teched off" Germans with his Enfield the way he had so often killed turkeys back home; only now the stakes were bigger and, to York's delight, so were the targets. With machine gun fire clattering over his head and angry soldiers shouting orders, York sat calmly in the mud and scanned his front. When an enemy head popped up for a better look, York shot it.[19]

After several minutes, however, the Germans managed to approximate York's position and decided to rush him with bayonets. Knowing York was firing from a five-round clip, a lieutenant and five others jumped up and charged, ignoring the prisoners who waved at them to go back. The Germans apparently reasoned that at least one should be able to reach him before he could reload, but York, now on his feet and shooting "off-hand," used the pistol instead. As the Germans ran toward him, York once again drew on the instincts of a Tennessee hunter and shot the last man, then the fifth, and so on. Back home, York killed wild turkeys starting from the back so the others would not realize what was happening and scatter. Similarly, he realized that if he shot the lead man first, the others "would drop down and pump a volley into me and get me." York later remembered he "[g]ot the lieutenant right through the stomach and he dropped and screamed a lot. All the boches who were hit squealed just like pigs." His barrel hot and ammunition low, York turned back to the rifle and began to shout at the survivors to surrender.[20]

While York's attention was concentrated on the hillside, Vollmer fired his pistol at him repeatedly from across the clearing but could not hit him. Finally he decided he had seen enough. Approximately twenty Germans were dead, and York had survived a machine gun barrage, a bayonet assault, and Vollmer's own attempts to kill him, without missing a shot. Now the lieutenant stood up and called out "English?" York replied, "No, not English." "What?" Vollmer asked. "American," York answered. The German muttered, "Good Lord," and then offered to surrender his men. York leveled the automatic at his head and told him to do it.[21]

In his report on this incident to the German government, Vollmer declared he had resisted fiercely "until I was surrounded and—alone." He concluded, "I had no choice but to surrender." A single American soldier then pointed a pistol at him and marched him off into captivity. This version, however, was disputed by the other German witnesses who unanimously agree that Vollmer was not taken away by himself. York says the now-cooperative battalion commander blew a whistle, the firing ceased, and the gunners began to file down the hill with hands raised. Clearly Vollmer, as a German officer, could not admit to such an act. None of the German witnesses, perhaps conveniently, remembered hearing Vollmer blow a whistle as York described, but in whatever manner, Vollmer obviously indicated to his subordinates that they should throw down their arms. York underscored the point when one of the Germans ignored the order and lobbed a small grenade at him. The throw missed, and York shot the man.[22]

Although York had won his incredible shoot-out with the machine guns, he still faced a nearly impossible situation, isolated behind enemy lines, burdened with several dozen prisoners, and left with only seven able-bodied men besides himself. When one American said their predicament was hopeless, York snarled at him to be quiet and began organizing the prisoners for the return to American lines. The suspicious Vollmer, who had once worked in Chicago and spoke excellent English, asked York how many men he had, and the Tennessean allowed he had "a-plenty." He ordered the Germans to pick up the American wounded and then put his prisoners in double file with three Americans on each side and another at the rear of the column. Using Vollmer and two other officers in the party as cover, York made a "middler" of himself at the front. The idea came from a marble game popular among mountain children called "ring man" in which four marbles were placed in a square surrounding a fifth marble called a "middler."[23]

With his strange column arranged, York's next problem was choosing the best way to return. He put the question to Vollmer who pointed toward a gully angling off behind them. Realizing that the officer would try to deceive him, York marched the column in the opposite direction toward the front of the German position. Because York and his men had actually captured a rear echelon, as they moved in the direction of the American positions they encountered still more machine gun emplacements. One such unit was commanded by Lieutenant Thoma of the Seventh Bavarian Sapper Company. Placed at Vollmer's disposal on the night of October 7, the Sappers had moved into position early the next morning. On his way to the front, Thoma had noticed "the indifference and lack of precaution" on the part of the 210th Reserve Infantry as its men relaxed in the rear. Thoma centered his men on a machine gun perched atop some high ground and added one or two other light machine guns to the nest. Hearing lively rifle fire behind him, Thoma reconnoitered and found German soldiers in the process of surrendering to an American patrol. Quickly collecting a few men, he ran toward the doughboys, but Vollmer saw him and shouted, "It is useless, we are surrounded." He told Thoma to surrender. Startled by the order of his superior officer, Thoma said he would do so only on Vollmer's authority. The lieutenant dropped his belt and joined York's growing line of prisoners.[24]

Some Germans became York's prisoners almost by accident. A platoon commander with the Fourth Company of the 120th Landwehr, alarmed by the intense firefight behind him, slipped off to investigate and abruptly found himself under American guns. Another officer, Vollmer's adjutant, Lieutenant Glass, was rushing back from the front to report to the battalion commander when he "was suddenly surrounded by a number of Americans." Even ten years later, Glass could say, "I still have in my mind a fairly clear picture of the American soldier in charge," a memory sharpened because "it was he who kept his pistol aimed at me." His captor was "a large and strong man with a red mustache, broad features and . . . freckled face." Undoubtedly Glass was describing Alvin York.[25]

As the column moved forward, York, constantly threatening Vollmer, captured position after position. Only one gunner refused to give up, forcing York to kill him. By the time York reached the edge of the valley he had left just a few hours before, the hill was virtually free of Germans. Alarmed by the ominous silence, a neighboring German unit sent out a patrol which returned with word that "no trace of the Fourth Company could be found." Its support elements had also vanished. With the silencing of the guns, the fire on the Americans in the valley was substantially reduced and their advance began again. York's duel with the machine guns was the most spectacular part of his work that morning, but the systematic capture of the forward positions was vastly more important for the assault on the Decauville Railroad.[26]

One last problem York had anticipated did not develop. His column now included so many German prisoners that he feared American artillery would mistake them for a German counterattack and bombard them. As they moved down the slope of the hill, however, a command to halt rang out, and York found himself staring into the muzzles of a half-dozen doughboy rifles. Astounded by the story York told, the patrol escorted the outnumbered captors and their prisoners back to the safety of American lines.[27]

York reported immediately to battalion headquarters, where his startled superiors explained they did not have the facilities to detain such a large number of prisoners. At regimental headquarters he was told the same thing, so he was forced to move his flock a third time through intermittent shelling to division headquarters where the officers counted 128 enlisted men and 4 officers among his hunter's bag. His incredulous brigade commander stepped out of the command post and remarked to the corporal, "Well, York, I hear you have captured the whole damned German army." York saluted and said no, he only had 132.[28]

York marched out of the Argonne Forest and into the annals of American legend. In the midst of the greatest battle the U.S. Army had ever fought, a backwoods corporal from Pall Mall, Tennessee, had accomplished one of the most spectacular feats of individual heroism in the nation's history. Having acted virtually alone, he was credited with killing 25 Germans and capturing 132, and with putting thirty-five machine guns out of action while armed only with a rifle and a pistol. He was promoted to sergeant and showered with so many medals that York said he would have to wear two coats if he wanted to wear them all at the same time. Marshal Foch awarded him the French Croix de Guerre and told him, "What you did was the greatest thing accomplished by any private soldier of all the armies of Europe." The United States gave him the Distinguished Service Cross immediately and a few months later, after a thorough investigation of the incident, bestowed on him the Medal of Honor. Even tiny Montenegro, which York had probably never heard of, gave him a medal.[29]

The events of October 8, 1918, made Alvin York an American hero, but many details of what happened on the fog-shrouded morning in the Argonne are lost in the tumult of war. The men who were there later recalled a scene of wild confusion and violent death. Unfortunately, their memories reflected the chaos of the moment, making it almost impossible to reconstruct the situation exactly. Although the army collected affidavits from several participants just a few months after the incident, in 1929, when Captain Henry Swindler began to study the fight for the Army War College, he discovered that "the statements of various people concerned are quite conflicting." The frustrated researcher found it nearly impossible even to prepare a map because he had "not been able to place accurately the different phases of the action." While Captain Swindler's remarks referred to American accounts, German participants also gave highly contradictory versions of the incident, stories which naturally tended to minimize any embarrassment to themselves or to German arms.[30]

Most of the information about York's fight was collected by American sources in 1919 and by German investigators in 1929. Incredulous American officers, including Major Buxton and Captain Danforth, joined in gathering sworn statements from participants who provided rough sketches of events as they had perceived them. These documents plus York's war diary formed the basis for the account York published in 1928 as part of the autobiography he wrote with Tom Skeyhill. The next year, Captain Henry Swindler used the same material to orchestrate a reenactment of the shoot-out for the Army War College. Every account of York's life since then has accepted that description of events in largely uncritical fashion.[31]

The German version of what happened on October 8 was not written until 1929, when a German citizen living in Stockholm saw a story about York's feat in a Swedish newspaper. Outraged at what he considered an insult to his nation's armed forces, he sent the article to the German minister of war with the suggestion it be investigated, a task eventually delegated to the government records office, the Reichsarchiv. The office obtained written statements from twenty-two soldiers who had seen service west of Châtel-Chéhéry that day and prepared a detailed account, which disagreed with the American story in several respects. Although the German version provided some valuable new information, it has some serious flaws as a piece of evidence. First of all, the document was not prepared until ten years after the events being discussed, more than enough time for human memories to begin to falter. Second, as defeated men explaining their actions to their government, the Germans had a personal stake in justifying their conduct and probably their testimony was skewed accordingly. Perhaps the most damaging point against the German version, however, is that First Lieutenant Vollmer was permitted to rewrite his report after studying the accounts of his colleagues. The conclusions of the investigators, prepared under the title "The Origins of War Legends," are thus an exercise in self-justification to some degree; nevertheless the paper offers an important perspective on an obscure and confusing episode.[32]

Collectively, the German witnesses conceded York was a fine soldier, but they believed he grossly exaggerated his achievements on October 8. According to scholars at the Reichsarchiv, York "was a brave and fearless soldier" whose exploit "shows no more courage than thousands of German leaders of raiding parties exhibited before him." The Germans insisted that York and his companions were only a few of a great many Americans attacking their rear that morning. They found no evidence proving that York killed all of the twenty-five men whose bodies were found on the wooded hillside, nor did they believe York silenced thirty-five machine guns. One officer insisted there were not thirty-five guns in that sector, and the report concluded that York's count was inflated by adding destroyed guns that had been abandoned in the woods. No German mentioned York's shoot-out with the machine gunners and several flatly denied his story about killing six men with a pistol as they charged him. As for the remarkable total of prisoners York collected, the German report said York simply claimed as his own prisoners who had actually been captured by other units and then assembled at a central point under York's guard.[33]

The Reichsarchiv report then went on to accuse American soldiers of commiting war crimes against the prisoners. Insisting there was "no instance in which a German so brutally violated International Law," the report condemned York for threatening to kill Vollmer if he did not cooperate. Moreover, according to Lieutenant Glass, other Americans later announced they intended to shoot all their prisoners when they reached American lines. They drew their pistols and put some men against a tree, but suddenly another American appeared and interrupted the process. The new arrival then began to interrogate Vollmer while another doughboy cut off Vollmer's shoulder straps and stole his Iron Cross. Such attempts to terrorize captives, the Germans contended, were clear violations of international law.[34]

Assessing the accuracy of the Reichsarchiv report is a difficult matter. The publicity surrounding the York incident was an embarrassment to the nation's military tradition, and the German government obviously hoped to discredit the sergeant's account of it. Angered because "the German soldier is pictured as a pitiful and miserable creature," the Germans labeled York a "braggart" and a "liar." Vollmer derided York's story as "the product of a typically American megalomania." Yet at the same time, there is clearly a certain awkwardness in these vigorous denials. Most of the former officers who submitted statements to the investigators took pains to emphasize the fighting quality of their troops, even though the Reichsarchiv admitted "our fighting power in those days was no longer quite as splendid" as the ex-soldiers claimed. Vollmer himself ignored repeated requests for information from the Reichsarchiv before reluctantly coming in person to submit his report. After examining statements from Lieutenant Kuebler and Lieutenant Glass, however, both of whom offered mild criticism of Vollmer's conduct, the battalion commander "thought it best to make some changes in his own statement," a version he then spent two weeks preparing. "The fact that First Lieutenant Vollmer hesitated several months before making his report," the Reichsarchiv concluded, "may be regarded as a sign that he does not consider himself entirely without blame."[35]

The main thrust of the German argument is that "Sergeant York is not entitled to all this glory." Besides contending that there were not thirty-five machine guns on the left of the German front that morning, the Germans also admitted to losing only 213 men as prisoners that day. Consequently, they said, York's claims could not possibly be true. If one soldier captured 132 men, surely the rest of the Americans put together would capture more than 81. A letter from the commander of the 328th Infantry filed in 1918, however, disputes both of these figures. Writing to General Duncan, Lieutenant Colonel Richard Wetherill praised the work of the Second Battalion and credited it with seizing 123 machine guns and taking 350 prisoners in the assault on the Decauville Railroad. If the American statistics are more nearly correct, then York's count of guns and captives seems to be much more reasonable. Moreover the reports of the Germans themselves lend credence, at least, to the 132 figure. Lieutenant Kuebler estimated that Vollmer had approximately 85 soldiers with him in the rear area when Early and his patrol broke out of the woods. Lieutenant Glass, the man who recalled York so vividly, estimated the Americans had 80 prisoners when he was captured. Lieutenant Thoma admitted surrendering himself and "a few" of his men to York's column as it advanced toward American lines. Thus the testimony of these German officers tacitly acknowledges the possibility that York captured 90 men. York claimed to have captured four officers, and four officers—Vollmer, Glass, Kuebler, and Thoma—admit they were captured that morning under circumstances similar to those described by York. Indeed, Glass mentions a fifth officer he saw among the prisoners. None of this, of course, proves that York actually captured all thirty-five machine guns or took precisely 132 prisoners, but the evidence indicates that such totals are very close to the truth.[36]

More difficult to gauge is the assertion that twenty-five Germans died before York's rifle in the celebrated firefight. The Germans insisted that no such duel took place; the gunners began firing but stopped when the prisoners called to them, and York was never the target of a rush by a lieutenant and several enlisted men. The German account has an interesting omission, however. After the sappers ceased firing, they were "driven toward us into the ravine. . . . " None of the German witnesses explained why a fully armed machine gun nest occupying high ground should suddenly and meekly surrender. In contrast, virtually all the Americans present remembered seeing York firing at the sappers, and one man saw a small party charge him. York may or may not have killed all the men later found on the hillside, but his actions are the only available explanation for the surrender of the gunners.[37]

One final German criticism of York's story centered on the number of Americans who were behind German lines on the morning of October 8. Most German witnesses insisted there were dozens, even hundreds, of doughboys infiltrating their positions, overwhelming the Germans by sheer numbers. American accounts of the day's action cast considerable doubt on this assertion. For one thing, the Second Battalion actually attacked with its left flank in the air because the 328th Infantry did not receive word of a last minute ten-degree change in the direction of the attack. The runner carrying the message was killed, and his body was not discovered and the message delivered until nearly noon. A gap thus opened between the 328th and elements of the Twenty-eighth Division to the left. Furthermore, the Twenty-eighth advanced very slowly, leaving, as Captain Danforth said, "a considerable part of our front . . . uncovered." Certainly the members of York's patrol believed they were alone behind enemy lines and did not report seeing friendly forces. Whatever the Germans thought they saw at the time or wanted to remember later, only a few Americans could have been operating behind their left flank in the hours after the doughboys started down Hill 223.[38]

Over the years, York's story has encountered some criticism from American sources as well as German. Even before York landed in the United States, a few members of his patrol were suggesting they deserved credit too, despite their sworn statements that they had done little more than "guard prisoners." Asked about these complaints, York simply said, "They raised their right hands and swore to those affidavits." Some students of the event argued that Bernard Early was the real hero of the day. Irked because York "has drummed up and down the country as a one-man army," a member of the patrol pointed out that Early had "used his head in getting his platoon into the woods without a casualty." Although

Early eventually received the Distinguished Service Cross, the Connecticut Department of the American Legion adopted a resolution asking Congress to award the New Haven man the Medal of Honor. A friend of Early's told the press, "It is a known fact among the boys in his outfit that Sergeant Early accomplished the feat for which Sergeant York has been credited."[39]

Such carping did little to shake York's version of events. Major General Duncan assured reporters in 1919, "The more we investigated the exploit the more remarkable it appeared. He is one of the bravest of men and entitled to all the honor that may be given to him." An Army War College inquiry conducted ten years later reached the same conclusion. As late as 1935, Captain Danforth insisted,"Credit was given where credit was due." Grievously wounded in the first barrage from the machine gunners, Early played little part in the actual fighting that won York the medal. His backers were certainly correct in claiming some credit for Early, but York plainly carried the burden of the battle. As for other discontented members of the patrol, York rightly pointed out that their own affidavits, taken before the incident attracted publicity, indicated they had contributed little to the fight. Moreover, as a *New York Times* editorial noted, neither York nor the army claimed he had achieved the feat singlehandedly. The Medal of Honor citation commends York for "fearlessly leading seven men" against a machine gun nest. In the final analysis, no convincing evidence exists that York received credit that should have gone to another man.[40]

Nevertheless, even some who accept York's version as true have suggested that his achievement was really less remarkable than it seemed because the Germans were eager to surrender as defeat drew nearer. A little evidence supports this view. The fighting effectiveness of the Second Landwehr and the Forty-fifth Reserve was clearly deteriorating and morale was very bad. At noon on October 8, just a few hours after York returned from his mission, Captain Danforth and his company runner surprised forty-four Germans who surrendered without firing a shot. Admittedly enemy resistance was weakening, yet the members of the Second Battalion pinned down below Hill 223 would have found it hard to believe that declining morale was a problem in the German army. Certainly the machine gunners York faced, who killed or wounded half of his patrol, did not seem eager to surrender. Nine Americans and over twenty Germans lay dead or wounded by the time Vollmer ordered a cease-fire. Even then, two prisoners attempted to pick York off but missed. The official report of the Eight-second Division concerning the action of October 8-9 spoke of "resistance of a very savage character and most destructive enemy machine gun and artillery fire." By midnight on October 9, York's 328th Infantry Regiment was down from its official strength of 112 officers and 3,720 enlisted men to 36 officers and 1,053 enlisted men. The savagery of the fighting is illustrated by General Duncan's account of an officer of the 328th who found a dead doughboy and a dead German soldier lying beside the De-cauville Railroad, each stabbed through with the other's bayonet.[41]

In the final analysis, it is clear that a number of factors contributed to York's striking success in the Argonne. Most important was York's own military skill. Accidents of terrain and position made it possible for a single rifleman to be highly effective against much greater firepower, and York's long experience with weapons enabled him to exploit fully his advantage over the machine gunners. His task was made easier by the carelessness of the men of the 210th Reserve, which allowed the Americans to compromise the rear of the German position in the first place. From the moment Early's patrol broke out of the woods, the Americans never really lost the initiative in the battle. Moreover, Lieutenant Vollmer clearly panicked. So rattled that he emptied his pistol at York without hitting him, Vollmer then abandoned all resistance and completely surrendered his sector of the line. Certainly the Germans should have been able to overwhelm York, but, as Vollmer's actions indicate, they were exhausted, confused, and frightened. They could not match an inspired marksman who believed God was with him.[42]

Although the army saw York as a good soldier and the press would soon portray him as a hero, York labored to understand what had happened on his own terms. The horror of October 8 hit him hard. His best friend, Corporal Murray Savage, died in the first blast from the guns on the slope, his clothes shot to tatters by over a hundred rounds. As the column of prisoners moved out of the clearing, York caught a glimpse of his dead friend that stayed in his mind forever. Tortured by the thought that some might still be alive, the next day he secured permission from Danforth to take a detail back to the grisly scene to look for any wounded men who might have survived. York's anguish was increased by his belief that he had killed twenty-five human beings. He knelt on the battlefield and prayed for their souls just as he did for the Americans who had died. Forty years later, an ill, bedfast old man, he would twice ask his minister-son how God would view what he had done in the Argonne. Throughout his life, he said little about his combat experiences and certainly never took pride in the exploit that had brought him fame. At a dinner given for York after his return to the United States, General Duncan asked him to say a few words about the fight in the Argonne, but York politely begged off, explaining, "It is one of those things I want to forget."[43]

Gradually York came to see his victory over the machine guns as the fulfillment of God's promise that because he was serving in a holy cause, he would return to Pall Mall unharmed. When a reporter asked York in early 1919 how he could possibly have survived the ordeal, York replied, "We know there are miracles, don't we? Well this was one. I was taken care of—it's the only way I can figure it." Aware of York's religious background, the reporter then asked what Pastor Pile would think, and York answered, "What can he say? What can any of them say? 'Blessed is the peacemaker' isn't he? Well, there was sure some stir-up in this country." The more he thought about it, the more York saw his survival as the vindication of his faith. Ever since he had come down from the mountain after the long night of wrestling with his conscience, he had felt a divine hand on him. Not long after the Armistice was signed he told listeners, "Somehow I knew I wouldn't be killed. I've never thought I would be—never once from the time we started over here." Thus the regret he felt at so many dead was tempered by his faith that he had been the instrument of God in a sanctified cause. Asked why God had protected him while letting others die, York replied that he did not understand the ways of God; "I jes accept them and bow my head and bless His holy name, and believe in Him more'n ever."[44]

After the fight with the machine guns, York still faced three more weeks in combat. His unit continued to take heavy casualties throughout the Argonne offensive, and York himself had his closest brush with death when an exploding shell literally blew him into the air as he desperately dug a foxhole. On November 1, York was at last rotated into a rest area where he was promoted to sergeant for his heroism. He was on leave in Aix-les-Bain when the Armistice was signed on the eleventh. "And they sure was a time in that city that day and night," York remembered, but the new sergeant tasted little of it. He visited a church, wrote a note to his mother, and went to bed about sundown.[45]

4. An American Hero

"Hero-worship," Dixon Wecter has written, "answers an urgent American need." Through its heroes, this sprawling, heterogeneous nation tries to express its identity and come to terms with its most powerful experiences. As Robert Penn Warren put it, "to create a hero is to create a self." In 1919, the United States was desperately in need of a hero. For half a century, the nation had grappled with the Industrial Revolution, a far-reaching social and economic force that had relentlessly fashioned an urban, industrial society from what had been a land of farms and small towns. This economic upsurge had lured millions of people from Europe who were very different from the majority of native Americans in their language, religion, and customs. Simultaneously, it produced a more sophisticated, city-dwelling American who, while sneering at the rural America he considered beneath him, had not evolved a value system and a sense of identity to replace the one being destroyed by the new era.[1]

The Great War only added to this sense of disorientation. For the first time in history, American troops were sent to Europe to fight, an action that violated foreign policy precepts stretching back to George Washington and Thomas Jefferson. With his Fourteen Points and his call to "make the world safe for democracy," Woodrow Wilson managed to explain the war in terms of American ideals, but the country shuddered at the wrenching change of course for the ship of state. Moreover, warfare itself had been reshaped by the Industrial Revolution. World War I began at a time when technology was able to produce simpler weapons of defense but not the more complicated offensive weapons needed to challenge those defenses. Thus the war was dominated by clattering machine guns, each capable of spewing 450 rounds per minute into advancing assault waves. Such fire power presented awesome tactical problems for would-be attackers and moved Secretary of War Newton Baker to declare, "Perhaps no invention has more profoundly modified the art of war than the machine gun." The lengthening casualty lists from the Western Front brought to life the enduring spector of the industrial age, machines turning on their creator to dominate or destroy mankind. In short, war had become, to quote Baker, "an industrial art conducted like a great modern integrated industry," which left the individual soldier an anonymous role comparable to that of an assembly line worker.[2]

The fears and uncertainties within American society spawned the Red Scare of 1919. Throughout the war, many Americans had feared that the nation's large immigrant population would prove disloyal to the war effort, so the government had created the Committee on Public Information under George Creel to explain and interpret the conflict for the American people. Unfortunately, the committee was guilty of a number of excesses that ignited a hatred of all things foreign. When the war abruptly ended, Americans simply transferred their aggressions to newer and nearer dangers than German militarism. Early 1919 saw a sharp upsurge of radical activity in the United States that alarmed many people. In January a general strike paralyzed the city of Seattle, and the spring brought a series of terrorist bombings aimed at such major political and business leaders as Attorney General A. Mitchell Palmer and oil baron John D. Rockefeller. These events seemed especially ominous in light of the successful communist revolution in Russia. Thus, although there was little reason to suspect a bolshevik conspiracy, the ambitious Palmer established an antiradical division in the Justice Department under future FBI director J. Edgar Hoover and set out to win the presidency in 1920 by manipulating the public's exaggerated fear of radicals and foreigners.[3]

Unaware of the troubled mood back home and the consequences it held for him, York spent the winter of 1918-19 in
France receiving decorations, performing Christian service,
and doing public relations work for the army. On Christmas
Day, he was dispatched to Paris to meet President Wilson.
Despite the fact that they were both products of the southern
Appalachians, the Tennessee blacksmith and the Virginia-
born university president could hardly have been more
dissimilar. The lean, reserved Wilson who bore himself with
the air of a scholar contrasted sharply with the husky sergeant
and his casual, gregarious manner. Preoccupied with the
details of the peace, Wilson cared little for soldiers of any rank
or achievement, so York was politely dismissed after a few
moments of bland conversation; but while the president
pondered the fate of millions, York faced a more immediate
concern. At no time during the day did Wilson or anyone else
offer him a bite of Christmas dinner, a discourtesy no holi-
day guest would have had to endure in Fentress County. After
the New Year, York concentrated on revival work. For six
weeks, he and the division chaplain rode automobiles and
motorcycles to prayer meetings with small groups of soldiers
assembled in YMCA huts, or sometimes open fields, sessions
that helped to spark a revival that swept through the Eight-
second during the winter. York eagerly took the post of choir
leader at the services in preparation for resuming similar
duties back home.[4]

Anxious as he was to return to Pall Mall, York was
charmed and fascinated by Paris. His first chance to see much
of the city came in March 1919, and he returned a month later
to attend the organizational meeting of the American Legion.
On both trips he walked the streets endlessly, visiting such
places as Versailles and the tomb of Napoleon. Since he had
never heard of an opera before entering the army, he went
to see one, knowing only that it was music, "a lot of them
stringed instruments playing together." He was surprised by
the four-dollar admission charge, and probably by some other
things as well, but, "I sat through it all right. I like the or-
chestra, but I don't think I'd ever again spend four dollars to
see another opera like it." Whatever its odd customs, the city

won the veteran hunter's respect in a very practical way. Walking its streets, York became lost for one of the few times in his life. Every avenue ran into a dead end, the buildings were all strange, and the names were mysterious. Even checking the sun did not help him get his bearings. Finally he gave up and asked directions of a "mademoiselle" who led him to a streetcar and told the "mademoiselle conductor" where to put him off. Though York toured several French cities, Paris remained his favorite. During an interview in Chattanooga on his way home, he told a reporter," . . . if you haven't been there you're lucky, because if you had been there you would be wantin' to go back."[5]

Somewhat surprisingly, the army played only a minor role in publicizing York's exploit in the Argonne and did little to bring him to the attention of the nation. One factor in this muted response to York may have been the cautious attitude of General John J. Pershing, commander of the American Expeditionary Force in France. Although Pershing is often quoted as labeling York the outstanding soldier of the war, a careful search by a group of competent historians in 1967-68 failed to turn up evidence of such a statement, and it is unlikely he ever made it. Pershing's reluctance to tout York probably had at least two dimensions. First of all, available evidence indicates that his personal choice of an individual as the outstanding soldier of the war was Samuel Woodfill, a regular army sergeant given a reserve commission when the war broke out, who singlehandedly silenced five machine gun nests on October 12. In his final report to the War Department, Pershing cited York, Woodfill, and Major Charles Whittlesey of the "Lost Battalion" as outstanding examples of American gallantry. In a private letter, however, Pershing implicitly compared the three and ascribed to Woodfill "the highest type of heroism" while describing the feats of the other two in less extravagant terms.[6]

Moreover, as Pershing fully realized, he faced a painful public relations problem in this area. The relatives of soldiers who had died in the war all naturally considered their kinfolk heroic. Pershing received a poignant reminder of this fact after his final report became public when he received a sad letter from a father whose son had been killed at Belleau Wood. Irked by Pershing's list of heroes, the writer admonished Pershing that "the boys who gave their lives are the great heroes" and assured the general that "my feelings are the feelings of the Mothers and Fathers of this country when you pick out one man and proclaim him the greatest hero." Pershing's aide, Colonel George C. Marshall, prepared a tactful reply for his own signature, but Pershing decided the issue was too important for a subordinate and signed the letter himself.[7]

To avoid such wounded feelings, the service carefully refrained from attaching superlatives to York or any other soldier. Of course the army awarded York the Distinguished Service Cross and the Medal of Honor, but the ceremonies and press releases attached no particular significance to his feat. At times, in fact, the AEF seemed to be taking pains to avoid giving York special treatment. Although plans were underway to give York a huge welcome in New York and Washington, he and sixty-one others were crowded off the ship on which their unit was scheduled to sail and were forced to wait until another vessel sailed the next day.[8]

York's fame was largely the product of press attention, especially from the *Saturday Evening Post*. In 1919 the *Post* claimed a circulation in excess of two million, the largest in the world, and was probably the nation's most influential periodical. Under its editor, George Lorimer, the *Post* "reflected the United States to itself." Lorimer favored stories that expressed in words the image of a patriotic, innocent, decent America that the young artist Norman Rockwell was beginning to portray on the cover of the magazine. When the war broke out, the prosperous *Post* sent a veteran journalist named George Pattullo to Europe to cover the AEF. It was Pattullo who stumbled onto the York story, recognized its potential, and went to interview him on the battle site.[9]

Pattullo discovered the York story by accident. Touring the Argonne a few weeks after the Armistice, the journalist got his initial tip from an anonymous traveling companion.

Shortly afterward, York's battalion commander, George Buxton, himself a journalist, also passed along the suggestion that the York story was worthwhile, so Pattullo decided to pursue it. He spent three days with York and his buddies, going over every foot of the terrain in the Argonne. A shrewd reporter, Pattullo realized the sensational value of his find, but he faced a potentially serious problem. Because censorship was still in effect, the army had to review his story before he could forward it to the *Saturday Evening Post*. The *Post* would need six weeks after delivery to publish the piece, and Pattullo was afraid his scoop would leak to the newspaper correspondents who literally could publish it overnight. Pattullo approached General Dennis E. Nolan, Pershing's chief of intelligence, explained his predicament, and asked him to take the matter up with General Pershing. Instead, Nolan decided to handle the situation himself. He told Pattullo he would not suppress material if other reporters discovered York, but he guaranteed the censors would not leak Pattullo's article.[10]

Six anxious weeks later, Pattullo's article appeared in the *Post* issue of April 26, 1919, and instantly catapulted York to prominence. Prior to its publication, no newspapers, not even in Tennessee, had taken notice of him, and York himself had not yet told his family about the events in the Argonne. Pattullo puckishly noted, "Newspapers learned of it from the *S. E. Post* . . . ," and he gained "a lot of publicity I didn't bother to read because I never valued it." Pattullo also claimed the York story gave him a *coup* at the expense of General Pershing. The AEF commander "got sore at me because he had a regular army sergeant he wanted to exalt as [the] real individual hero of the war." According to Pattullo, army headquarters later issued the story, obviously Woodfill's, "but the achievement could not touch York's, and the story was cold and routine."[11]

Pattullo's treatment of the story cast York in a heroic mold and laid the basis for the York legend. The title, "The Second Elder Gives Battle," suggested the characteristics of the Christian warrior that York came to personify. Pattullo discussed

at length York's deep religious faith and how it had changed
his life in 1915 and had given him deep doubts about the
morality of soldiering. At the same time he stressed York's
ability with firearms and compared him to a Western gun-
fighter. As a result, the York whom Pattullo described seemed
to reflect a fundamental ambivalence in the American
character. Although Americans pride themselves on being a
peace-loving people, they often idolize violent men. The First
World War brought this ambivalence to the surface in that
the public took pride in the role its army played in the fighting
even though Americans did not really understand the war
itself. York meshed neatly with both the traditional American
character and with public attitudes about the war by being
a reluctant but highly successful soldier.[12]

Another theme in Pattullo's article centered on his portrayal of York as an Appalachian mountain man. The journalist placed York squarely in the midst of a popular set of
stereotypes about Appalachia. As historian Henry Shapiro has
written, around the turn of the century, Americans began to
develop contradictory attitudes about the region. The source
of this dichotomy was the Industrial Revolution, which was
rapidly destroying the old rural America and replacing it with
a new, urbanized society geared to mass production. Amid
such rapid change, Americans worked to create a new order
while they simultaneously expressed nostalgia for the old one.
Hence, in one sense Appalachia was a tragic aberration within
the American success story because its poverty and isolation
contrasted sharply with the prevailing notion that industrialization and urbanization were the standards of economic
progress. According to this view, the typical mountain man
was violent and antisocial in his behavior, ever ready to start
a family feud or shoot a revenue agent. A countervailing idea
that appeared at almost the same time cast Appalachia as the
last repository of the vanishing traditions that supposedly
were "truly American"—individualism, hard work, and the
English legacy in politics and culture. From this perspective,
a mountaineer was slow to anger yet skillful with weapons,
plainspoken, religious, patriotic, and something of a child of

nature who, despite his innocence and lack of sophistication, naturally did the right thing.[13]

The York whom Pattullo introduced to the country represented the latter notion. Patriotism, Pattullo assured his readers, "was stronger in the Tennessee mountains than any other impulse." The Enfield rifle and .45 pistol became "particularly American weapons," and the "big redhead is sure death with either," although Pattullo quickly added that "they won't stand for moonshining or lawlessness in Pall Mall." York's "unflustered" manner and "unhurried, half-indolent" gait reflected "absolute sureness of self." Answers to the journalist's questions came back "like the crack of a whip." Pattullo marveled that the poorly educated "Tennessee mountaineer seems to do everything correctly by intuition" and quoted army officers saying "no amount of military training could have improved his tactics" but the unschooled York had acted entirely by "instinct." In Pattullo's hands, York became the frontiersman reincarnated in the machine age not only to slay the enemies of the republic but also to reaffirm the validity of traditional American values in a time of upheaval.[14]

If the legend of Sergeant York, as designed by George Pattullo, reinforced certain stereotypes about Appalachia, it also marked an important stage in the development of the "idea" of Appalachia. Industrialization fostered the belief that America was, or should be, a unified and homogeneous society with a uniform culture. In this context, the apparent "otherness" of that "strange land inhabited by a peculair people" was troubling because this white Anglo-Saxon Protestant area seemed so at variance with the dominant cultural norms that other white Anglo-Saxon Protestants eagerly embraced. This apparent contradiction was eventually resolved in the early twentieth century by a new perception of both America and Appalachia. The notion of a homogeneous culture gradually gave way to a view of American civilization as pluralist in tone and committed to diversity. Also, the concept took hold that the "peculiar people" of Appalachia represented a legitimate subculture within that disparate society.[15]

The celebration of Sergeant York in 1919 marked the culmination of this process: for the first time a mountaineer was acclaimed as such away from his native ground. Prior to this time, as Shapiro has noted, "Mountaineers who left the mountains ceased being mountaineers," but the full emergence of the idea that Appalachia was a distinct place with a distinct culture meant that the mountaineer would carry his unique traits with him wherever he went. Thus, whether he was in France or Tennessee, Alvin York remained a child of the mountains. Consequently, York became part of a new mythic pattern in American society. He was never simply an American hero but rather was preeminently a mountaineer. Indeed the sense of "otherness" connected with Appalachia was so strong that York was never connected with any of the powerful myths of the South, even though he was a Tennessean and the Civil War was barely fifty years in the past. Instead he became the near-perfect symbol of a new character, the independent mountaineer.[16]

The blend of Christianity and patriotism that Pattullo ascribed to York made the sergeant an important part of what sociologist Robert Bellah has labeled the American civil religion. Since the days of the Founding Fathers, Bellah argues, Americans have drawn on the Judeo-Christian faith to explain the nation's role in history. In his words, the civil religion "is not the worship of the American nation but an understanding of the American experience in the light of ultimate and universal reality." Its interpretations rooted in the Bible, the civil religion suggests that God is active in history and has made Americans His "chosen people" whom He delivered from British bondage in the Revolution just as He delivered the ancient Israelites from Egypt. Like that of the Israelites, America's destiny was to be the instrument of God's will in history by serving as a light to the corrupt nations of the Old World.[17]

According to Bellah, the travail of the Civil War simultaneously confirmed this view of America and added another dimension to the civil religion. The sectional strife and eventual triumph of the Union brought themes of sacrifice, death, and rebirth that were inspired by the gospel accounts of the passion of Jesus. For example, in his Gettysburg Address, Abraham Lincoln used the biblical concept of redemptive suffering in extolling the war dead. Later, through his own tragic martyrdom, Lincoln came to embody the idea he had so eloquently expressed. As Washington became the American Moses, so Lincoln became the American Christ. Despite the agony the Civil War brought, therefore, the fiery ordeal purified the nation and proved it had the character and fortitude to carry out God's plan.[18]

York's understanding of World War I and America's role in it corresponded well with the basic tenets of this civil religion. He believed in the superior morality of the Allied cause and was convinced that America was fighting on God's side against German perfidy. Indeed, he had taken up arms only when he was convinced of the righteousness of America's action. According to this view, American intervention was simply part of God's plan to redeem the world through His chosen people, and Alvin York had served as one of the Lord's agents in the Argonne Forest. Interestingly enough, York felt humbled rather than exalted by the role he believed God had picked him to play, a reflection of a faith that genuinely stressed the need for Christians to serve God as well as their fellow man. Moreover, York believed that the terrible suffering he had witnessed was also part of God's plan and must be accepted as an integral part of redemption. Thus York not only presented a reassuring personal image to the American public, he also rationalized in simple and familiar terms a war most of his fellow countrymen found complex and terrifying.

The response to the Pattullo article was enormous. As the journalist himself put it years later, "I would recommend the way 'The Second Elder Gives Battle' was built up, and handled, to all young aspiring writers under 70." The Tennessee Society, a group of prosperous former Tennesseans then living in New York, began laying plans to give York a spectacular welcome when he docked. Working through York's congressman, Cordell Hull, they arranged a five-day furlough to show York New York and Washington, D.C. The Nashville

Banner dispatched a reporter to Pall Mall to file a series of stories on York's family and background. In Jamestown, local banker William L. Wright hastened out to the York homestead to read the magazine story to the family. An overjoyed Mary York asked him to read it seven times before Wright could excuse himself.[19]

York landed at Hoboken, New Jersey, on May 22 and was met at the dock by members of the society and a crowd of reporters. He had been informed that a celebration was planned in his honor, but he was not prepared for the extravaganza the society had outlined under the slogan, "York Must See New York and New York Must See York." After a brief welcome and some questions from the press, he was loaded into a car and driven through a ticker tape blizzard to his room at the Waldorf-Astoria. York did not quite realize what was happening. As he admitted, the cheering crowds "plumb scared me to death," and he did not understand that the parade was for him until his new friends explained it to him. He had assumed every returning soldier got the same treatment.[20]

That evening the hero was the guest of honor at a formal banquet. York had had little experience with such affairs in Pall Mall, but he slyly kept his manners straight by watching others before he used the variety of utensils set before him. While a series of speakers praised his character and achievements, York's mind wandered constantly as he daydreamed about hunting in the mountains again. Much as he appreciated what the Tennessee Society had done, he could not hide his disappointment at being unable to reach his mother by a long-distance telephone call.[21]

Under the tutelage of the Tennessee Society, York spent the next few days visiting the usual New York and Washington tourist sites. Asked what he would most like to see in New York, he pondered a moment and decided on the subway. He had never heard of a subway before entering the army and was curious about it, so transit officials gave him a tour in a special car. That evening he boarded a train to Washington, where he was to be the guest of Congressman Hull on a tour of government offices. His appearance in the

House of Representatives brought a standing ovation which York acknowledged with a salute. He then had a brief meeting with Secretary of War Newton Baker and went from the War Department to the White House. Wilson was still in Paris but his secretary, Joe Tumulty, received the congressman and his constituent. At each place he was invited to discuss his exploits, but he persistently refused. In Tumulty's office he took a chair off to one side and left the politicians to chat with each other. Hull understood York's feelings and refused all other invitations, taking him instead on an automobile tour through Rock Creek Park. The following day he returned to New York for the last stop on his tour, the New York Stock Exchange. The Tennessean had no concept of a stock market and the whole visit "didn't mean nothing to me nohow" but, as always, he was polite and appreciative, though eager to get home.[22]

By May 28 York was at last on his way to Fort Oglethorpe, Georgia, for his final discharge. By the time the train reached Tennessee, he was again in the midst of a triumphal procession. A large crowd met him during a short layover in Knoxville and asked him to return for a formal welcome. The travel-weary soldier was noncommital, however, explaining, "I want to go home and see my mother first of all." He began his last day as a soldier with an early morning arrival in Chattanooga, where he was met by the commander of nearby Fort Oglethorpe and a committee of ladies who showered him with roses. Taken to a hotel to relax, York decided to get his hair cut. After finding so many things strange in New York, he had been reluctant to ask for one during his stay there, so he was startled when, that close to home, the hotel barber staff began giving him an elaborate cut, shampoo, and manicure. Partway through the process, curiosity overcame politeness and he asked what was happening. Finally, climbing out of the chair, he explained, "That is the first one of them I have ever had." Sounding not altogether convinced he pronounced the experience "not so bad." The general then took him to a Rotary Club dinner and from there to the spring festival at a city park. York especially enjoyed the roller coaster, but the high point of the day came late in the afternoon when the general handed him his discharge papers. He spent the night in Chattanooga and by early morning was making "wide tracks" for Pall Mall.[23]

Despite his eagerness, York's journey was slow because so many towns along the way wanted to honor him. In order to accommodate the greatest number of people, he took the train to Rockwood and then traveled by car to Harriman, making a Tennessee Central connection to Crossville where friends met him in automobiles. All six cars in Jamestown had made the fifty-mile trip to the station. Around seven o'clock that evening the little procession stopped in front of the Mark Twain Hotel in Jamestown and York went inside to meet his mother at last. The reunited family had a quiet supper at the hotel and then rode home together through the crisp evening air.[24]

Safely home, York's first project was to arrange a wedding. Early the next morning he was off to the Williams farm for a meeting with Gracie, and the following day, Sunday, June 1, he escorted her to Decoration Day services. Miss Williams was extremely shy and was unwilling to have her picture taken, until York finally coaxed her to permit it. They went for a ride in a "flivver" belonging to the Nashville *Banner* but refused to discuss their plans. On Wednesday, however, the *Banner* received a telegram from Pastor Pile announcing the couple would be married on Saturday with Governor Albert H. Roberts officiating. The wedding was preceded by a huge welcome home celebration at which Roberts and his political ally, the German-born owner of the *Banner*, E.B. Stahlman, gave testimonials to York. The ceremony began at noon with the couple standing on an immense rock beneath an American flag-draped arch. The brief service was then followed by a picnic lunch. Despite the adulation York received, his mother-in-law remained skeptical of the neighbor who was marrying her daughter. When a reporter commented that it was a great honor for her daughter to marry such a hero, Mrs. Williams sniffed, "Humph! So they tell me."[25]

On Monday, York and his bride left for the last of the

celebrations in his honor. Along with York's mother, the wedding party, and Pastor Pile, they went to Nashville as guests
of Governor Roberts for the state's official tribute to York.
The next day a thousand people jammed the governor's man-
sion for a reception, and that evening six thousand filled the
Ryman Auditorium to see Roberts award York a special state
medal. A delegation of women suffragists, eager to publicize
their case as the battle over the Nineteenth Amendment took
shape, also presented the new Mrs. York with a cameo pin.
"They showed me a great time in New York," the sergeant
admitted, "but Nashville is there with the goods."[26]

York's hosts also took care to show the visitors some of
the city's diversions. The governor's wife took Gracie York
to the Castner-Knott department store for a shopping tour conducted by the manager. Mrs. York expressed some skepticism
of city wares, however. "I painted my face once for fun," she
admitted, using "something I found around the house, and
I thought I would never get it off. I don't think I'll try it again."
Even more discomfited was Pastor Pile. Invited to join the
others at the theater and a movie, Pile initially refused but
then, to his ultimate regret, changed his mind and attended.
He stared woodenly at the floor when a "high kicker" appeared on the stage, later telling his hosts politely but firmly,
"I don't think it was a proper place for a preacher to go." The
York party also visited the Parthenon and Andrew Jackson's
home, the Hermitage, where York posed beside the president's
tomb for photographers. At the end of the week, they returned to Pall Mall, and at last the cheering stopped.[27]

York now faced one of the most difficult periods of his life.
Even before he left New York, the acclaim and publicity that
had surrounded him had brought a deluge of offers to capitalize on his fame in a variety of ways. The New York *Herald*
offered him ten thousand dollars for a single article on his
experiences in France. A theatrical company offered him fifty-
two thousand dollars for a year in vaudeville, while another
newspaper offered fifteen hundred dollars a week for 104
weeks. A film company offered him fifty thousand dollars for
the rights to his life story and a royalty deal that promised

to yield one hundred fifty thousand dollars more. After he returned to Pall Mall the offers continued to pour in at the rate of fifty to seventy-five a week, including one from a coal company offering him fifteen thousand dollars a year for the use of his name in advertising. A gun manufacturer promised him two thousand dollars for firing a single shot from one of its rifles while a photographer took a picture. No one made a careful count, but the offers totaled between a quarter and a half million dollars.[28]

York was puzzled and perplexed by these overtures. He had never expected to make money from his military service, and once he had returned from overseas, "I jes wanted to be left alone to go back to my beginnings." The stage and film possibilities did not seriously tempt him. York shared the suspicions many rural Tennesseans had of such entertainment, and his facetious remark that he would look silly in "tights" covered a real fear of being exploited or made ridiculous in such a setting. The idea of endorsing a product he did not use offended his basic honesty. More importantly, York felt that commercializing his fame would compromise the high ideals he believed the war was fought to attain. He was convinced that the Allied cause was divinely blessed and felt that receiving money for serving such a cause would be like Judas taking the thirty pieces of silver.[29]

York's final decision to refuse all the offers reflected one of the basic traits of the society that produced him, namely, an indifference to money. Poverty was a harsh fact of life for many families in the southern Appalachians, so York, like many others, grew up valuing land or guns or character above money. To York, money was simply another tool, like a rifle or a hoe, that was used for a purpose but not sought for its own sake. Never rich, he had always gotten by, and the prospect of substantial wealth meant little to him.

Also difficult to handle were the pressures to lend his name and support to various causes. His trip to Nashville was studded with requests to use his visibility to further certain activities, usually of a civic or religious nature, and whenever possible, York tried to comply. As the governor escorted him through the state offices, York made a point of asking the highway department to speed construction of a promised road in Fentress County. He appeared at a state-sponsored "Own Your Own Home" display at which various politicians took turns extolling homeownership as the surest bulwark against bolshevism. He and Pastor Pile agreed to assist the Nashville black community in raising funds for a school.[30]

The one gift York did accept was a farm from the Nashville Rotary Club. Shortly after the *Post* article appeared, Edgar M. Foster, president of Nashville Rotary and business manager of the Nashville *Banner,* suggested that the club begin collecting money to give York a good farm in Fentress County. Pastor Pile endorsed the idea, saying, "I am sure that Brother York will appreciate what the club is doing for him. Don't think they could have done anything that would be more appreciated by our boy." Without York's knowledge, Rotary and the *Banner* began a public subscription drive to purchase a four hundred-acre tract owned by banker W.L. Wright. Their goal was to buy and stock the farm as a tribute to York. He was skeptical when told of these plans but finally agreed to accept the farm when in late 1919 the club made a $6,250 down payment on the twenty-five thousand dollar price. The title was made out to Rotary and the rest of the money was to be paid in four annual installments.[31]

A central figure in the acclaim York received in Tennessee was the owner and publisher of the Nashville *Banner,* E.B. Stahlman, who gave York extensive coverage in his newspaper, made speeches at the Pall Mall and Nashville celebrations, and was a prime sponsor of the move to give York a farm. Although no evidence exists of Stahlman's motives, it is possible that he, like many others, hoped to gain something by being associated with the hero. Stahlman was a German immigrant who had been the target of some of the xenophobia the war had produced. Rumors circulated that he had received money for propaganda purposes from the German government and that he had been saved from internment only by the intervention of Senator Kenneth McKellar. By vociferously proclaiming his admiration of York, Stahlman possibly hoped to counter the slurs on his loyalty.[32]

Understanding why York received the welcome he did in 1919 does much to explain the kind of country the United States was in the postwar period. Certainly York was not the only doughboy who had performed spectacularly in France. Besides Samuel Woodfill whose daring exploits had so impressed General Pershing, many others had also conducted themselves well under fire. Sergeant Harry J. Adams, armed only with an empty automatic pistol, captured some 300 prisoners. Sergeant Hercules Korgia, wounded and taken prisoner, persuaded 256 of his captors to surrender to him. Private Sterling Morelock and three others silenced five machine gun nests. In fact, a recent student of World War I has remarked that courage was so common in the Argonne that medals were almost cheap.[33]

Clearly York represented more than military glory to the thousands who gathered to cheer him. First of all, York seemed to be a reincarnation of pioneer America in the midst of the twentieth century. His old-fashioned values emphasizing family and church were quaint but appealing to an urban nation insecure in its newfound sophistication. The understated, unruffled manner he demonstrated in public appearances embodied the traits Americans favored in their male heroes. His skill with weapons only emphasized the image of York as a modern day frontiersman. Secondly, York was part of a tradition of citizen-soldiers that stretched back to the minutemen of the revolutionary period. Americans had long nurtured a suspicion of compulsory military training, standing armies, and professional soldiers. Instead, the United States prided itself on being a nation where every citizen was ready to volunteer for the common defense at a moment's notice. According to American lore, such soldiers had fought with Andrew Jackson against the British at New Orleans and stormed San Juan Hill under Theodore Roosevelt. York's native state won the nickname of the Volunteer State because so many Tennesseans, among them Alvin York's grandfather, flocked to the colors during the Mexican War. Even a man with military ambitions like George Washington was careful to present himself as a modern Cincinnatus eager to return to the plow when his homeland was again secure. During

World War I, however, this volunteer spirit had been shaken by the realities of modern war. The United States adopted the most comprehensive mobilization of manpower in its history and looked to professional soldiers to organize the victory. In the face of such an overwhelming military establishment, York's heroics seemed to suggest that the minuteman tradition was still viable, making him a much more appealing hero than a professional soldier like Samuel Woodfill. The shrewd career officer John J. Pershing fully understood the significance of this point; hence his displeasure with Pattullo who had celebrated the amateur and not the professional.[34]

A hero like York was especially comforting in 1919 for other reasons as well. Warfare, like so many things in society, had fallen under the sway of machines, multiplying the terrors of combat and depersonalizing soldiers just as the mass production assembly line depersonalized workers. York's individual triumph over the machine guns was an assertion of the final supremacy of the individual over the steel monster that man had created. A thoughtful Newton Baker summarized this feeling when he wrote,

> The individual soldier who emerges from the mass has measured strength not with a single antagonist, but with all the unseen and multiplied terrors which modern science and invention have concentrated around the individual. There is no longer the pomp and parade, the waving of flags and the call of trumpets; from first to last, modern war is a grinding, deadly business. It is often said that the glory and the opportunity for individual exploit have all been taken out of war, but every now and then circumstances still make the opportunity, and certainly one such was made when Sergeant York, with his little band, found himself surrounded by machine gun nests in Châtel-Chéhéry on October 8, 1918.[35]

In this context of the individual in the machine age, the adulation York received anticipated the reaction to Charles Lindbergh after his dramatic flight from New York to Paris in 1927. Like York, Lindbergh was acclaimed as a rugged individualist who had faced seemingly insurmountable odds alone. Poets, politicians, and reporters invoked the imagery of early America by describing Lindbergh as a pioneer exploring the new frontier of the air. Yet whatever his achievements, the commentators agreed, Lindbergh's greatest triumph lay in the quality of his character and his modest, unassuming manner. All these themes clearly highlighted the popular view of York as well as Lindbergh. This similiarity of interpretation grew out of the nation's efforts to reconcile its agrarian heritage with its industrial surroundings. Originally established as a fragmented, agricultural country, the United States traditionally extolled such rural values as localism, individualism, and self-reliance. The advent of industrialism, however, placed a new premium on other patterns of behavior—collectivism, regimentation, and organization— as the keys to success in the new order. World War I exacerbated the tension between these two images of America, because the demands of the conflict only increased the pressure for a more rigidly structured society that took even less notice of the individual. The feats of both York and Lindbergh seemed to reassert the older, more humanistic values over the dictates of the machine age.[36]

World War I also fed a tremendous hatred of all foreign influences, a hatred that lingered after the Armistice in the form of the Red Scare. Several public officials, most notably Attorney General Palmer, issued strident warnings about the spread of radical ideas that would undermine the "pristine" American system. Since York represented so many basic American values, he became a restatement of those ideals in a time of apparent threat from competing ideologies. Finally, York helped Americans to make sense of the Great War. He implicitly confirmed Woodrow Wilson's pledge of a "crusade" by declaring that the Allied cause had been divinely blessed and that his victory in the Argonne was a miracle. As York saw it, his heroism confirmed the claim that the war really was a struggle to "make the world safe for democracy."

Alvin York became a popular hero because within himself

he caught the contradictory nature of the American character. Americans consider themselves peace loving but respect men of action; York was a conscientious objector who became a war hero. Americans are materialistic but consider themselves idealists; York rejected wealth because the terms for accepting it violated his conscience. The celebration of Alvin York was really meant, in a larger sense, as a celebration of American life. Yet ironically the York mythology sounded one other contradictory note. The acclaim York received carried a hint of pessimism about America's future. As Lindbergh would be ten years later, he was praised because he appeared to embody old-fashioned qualities that had made America great, but now, allegedly, people with those qualities were very rare. The implication clearly was that most Americans in 1919 lacked the admirable qualities once so abundant among their heroic ancestors. If such were the case, the days of American glory were past, and our society was already on the road to collapse. Urbanization and industrialization were proving to be ultimately corrupting after all. But in 1919, such melancholy implications went largely unnoticed.[37]

5. The Hero at Home

Even more than most returning doughboys, Alvin York faced a difficult readjustment to home life. A reluctant draftee from a poor family in 1917, he returned to Pall Mall barely eighteen months later as an internationally famous war hero with dozens of lucrative opportunities spread before him. His position in the community was completely changed; the obscure day laborer was now the most prominent man in Fentress County. Convinced God had chosen him for a special work, York was determined to use his fame to benefit his native region. Ironically, however, the virtues the public thought it saw in Alvin York the hero—a self-reliant child of nature uncorrupted by cities or schools—were precisely the qualities that made it difficult for York to be successful in his peacetime enterprises. Too individualistic to cooperate with his opponents and too poorly educated to manage his responsibilities, York found that his background left him better prepared for his adventure in the Argonne than for a life of public service. Not surprisingly, therefore, the years after York's return to Pall Mall often brought him personal failure and public embarrassment. In many ways the civilian York seems to be a decidedly unheroic figure, but he never wavered in his commitment to use his own fame for the benefit of his friends and neighbors.

York's understanding of his homeland changed greatly while he was away. As he put it, "The big outside world I had been in and the things I fought through teched me up inside a most powerful lot. The old life I had lived seemed a long, long way behind me." Like many rural Southerners, he felt a strong sense of attachment to his native area, but now he was increasingly aware of the problems his people faced. Where he had once seen the mountains as "our shield against the iniquities of the outside world," now he realized they had also "kept out many of the good and worthwhile things like good roads, schools, libraries, and up-to-date homes, and modern farming methods."[1]

Just as he had during wartime, York linked his new point of view to his religious faith. He gradually came to the conclusion that God had chosen him to bring the benefits of industrial society to his neighbors, and that the war had simply been part of God's plan to prepare him for such a life of service. His travels had shown him the advantages of the modern world, while the horrors of combat had taught him to value human life. The "Greeks and Italians and New York Jews" of the polyglot Eighty-second Division had helped him to love and understand others. As a final test, God had made him famous and tempted him with glory and potential wealth in order to test his character. With all these trials behind him, York felt he was now ready for the work he believed God had set before him. "My ambition," he said," . . . is to devote my time to improving conditions here in the mountains."[2]

Besides his religious faith, York's commitment to public service also grew out of the values of the agrarian society that had nurtured him. Although York and his fellow mountaineers are often portrayed as "rugged individualists," the conditions of mountain life fostered a great deal of communal activity. Growing up in a society that obtained most of its power from the muscles of people and animals, York learned early that neighbors had to cooperate with each other. As one student of folk life on the Upper Cumberland puts it,

> More than any other word, *cooperation* is the key to understanding the life-style of the agricultural era. Every thought and every act was bound up in the concept of helping one another. Oral traditions testify that . . . the farm families of the Upper Cumberland perfected the art of cooperation and community living.

York and his friends realized the importance of self-reliance, but they also understood how vital it was for neighbors to assist each other. As he considered his plans for the future, York naturally drew on this basic trait of the society that produced him.[3]

Unfortunately, York's plans were hindered by personal financial trouble brought on partly by a farm depression. In the months after World War I, the nation's agricultural economy sank under the weight of immense surpluses. The government had encouraged expanded production during 1917 and 1918 to meet war needs, but as soon as the Armistice was signed, it withdrew from the market and simply let prices fall. Consequently, many farmers faced hard times as the 1920s began, but ironically Alvin York's problems were compounded by the land presented to him by the Rotary Club. Although the club had originally promised a fully equipped farm, what York actually received fell far short of that. The property had no buildings, not even a house, and York did not own enough equipment to work it properly. Lacking the capital to supply and operate the farm, he had to borrow three thousand dollars just to buy livestock and machinery. Unable to turn a profit in the slow market, York, his wife, and their new baby, Alvin, Jr., were still living with York's mother on the old family homestead two years after his return from Europe.[4]

York's situation became more ominous in the fall of 1921 when the note on the farm came due. While the Rotary Club had originally intended to pay the entire twenty-five thousand dollar cost of the farm, it had failed to raise enough money so it made an initial down payment of $6,250 with the rest to be paid in installments. The club met the first note of $4,687.50 in November 1920, but York was left to meet two other installments of equal size in 1921 and 1922 and a final payment of $2,687.50 in 1923. The latter was reduced by $2,000 because the owner of the property, Jamestown banker W.L. Wright, was contributing that amount to the farm fund. Unfortunately, by August 1921 it was obvious that York would not be able to pay the note without assistance. As he wrote in a desperate letter to Edgar M. Foster, general manager of the Nashville *Banner* and president of the Rotary

Club, "Since you all got me into this, I am trusting you will see me through and I believe you will."[5]

York's financial woes gave him his first bitter taste of the price of unsought adulation. In their poorly planned rush to reward York, the Rotary Club had actually created a major problem for him that was beyond his resources to manage successfully. He simply did not have the available capital or the business skill to take advantage of the gift. The farm was presented to him by people who admired York's self-reliance, but their gift undercut that self-reliance by putting York in a situation that was beyond his means to handle. Eventually he was forced to ask the Rotary Club for further assistance and then endure the humiliation of seeing his plight discussed extensively in the public press.

York's problems were not atypical, however, of the difficulties faced by a number of military heroes after World War I. At the same time the famous Tennessean was struggling to save his farm, another hero of the Argonne, Samuel Woodfill, found himself in similar straits. A career soldier, Woodfill reenlisted after the war to complete his time for retirement, but his meager army pay would not meet the mortgage payments on a farm he had purchased. Desperate, Woodfill took a leave of absence and hired out as a laborer to earn the money. He was digging ditches with a pipeline company when a reporter discovered his plight and wrote a story that prompted the Keith-Albee vaudeville tour to stage a series of benefits for him which paid off the eight thousand dollar debt in a few days. More tragic was the story of Major Charles Whittlesey, the commander of the "Lost Battalion" of the Seventy-seventh Division, a unit cut off from friendly forces for five days during the Argonne offensive. A shy man, Whittlesey was never able to come to terms with the unexpected and unwelcome public acclaim. "They're always after me about the war," he said. "I've got to help some soldier or other make some speech or something. I used to think I was a lawyer; now I don't know what I am." Haunted by the war he could not escape, Whittlesey committed suicide in November 1921.[6]

Faced with the possible embarrassment of seeing York lose the farm they had given him, the *Banner* and the Rotary Club once again launched a determined campaign to raise the money. Explaining that York was "simply caught like other farmers in a down market," the *Banner* pledged the first $50 toward the immediate goal of $4,687.50 and solicited donations in its columns. "To give him a $25,000 farm, with a mortgage of some $13,000, and expect him to do the rest," the *Banner* pointed out, "is very much of a gift without any real significance." The news stories about his plight brought York a sharp spate of criticism for his alleged financial mistakes. Rumors circulated that he was improvident as well as being a bad farmer. One story in particular claimed he had wastefully purchased a new Dodge, when actually the car had been a gift. York's refusal to commercialize himself in order to earn money also drew criticism. Simply being in debt, however, wounded York far more deeply than malicious gossip. "Before I went to the war I never owed any man a dollar I couldn't pay," he told a reporter. "I always worked hard, but I never worked harder than I do now, and the debts, as well as the raising of money to pay the help I must keep, are worrying me all the time. I could get used to most any kind of hardship, but I'm not fitted for the hardship of owing money."[7]

Efforts to raise the cash in Tennessee proved very frustrating, and York's farm was saved only after national publicity created wide sympathy for him. Although the *Banner* and the Rotary Club campaigned for weeks and attracted hundreds of contributors, the farm fund rose slowly because the agricultural depression kept most gifts very small. With the club barely able to meet the November deadline for the note, a discouraged Edgar Foster told York there was no chance of paying the 1922 note by popular subscription. Fortunately, people outside Tennessee who valued York as a symbol of patriotism also rallied to the cause, most importantly Marvin Campbell, a seventy-two-year-old Rotarian and bank president from South Bend, Indiana, who joined the York drive after reading an Associated Press account of the hero's plight.

Acting on his own initiative, Campbell sent a circular letter to ten thousand banks and sixty-five thousand Rotary Clubs across the country, explaining the situation and requesting a donation. Campbell's efforts netted approximately fifty-three hundred dollars toward paying the last two notes.[8]

The rest of the money came largely in response to an article about York written by New York *World* reporter E.J. Bruen, who traveled three days from the rail town of Livingston, Tennessee, to interview York in Pall Mall. Bruen stressed the difficulties York faced in getting his land into production and put to rest slurs about his incompetence and wastefulness. By pointing up the contrast between York's tumultuous homecoming and his current troubles, Bruen made the Tennessean a metaphor for the forgotten doughboy struggling in the peacetime recession. After the article appeared on December 4, 1921, a spontaneous nationwide drive began to "give York a Merry Christmas" by paying the remaining debt before December 25. W.N. Sharp, a Chicago businessman, offered $250 toward a goal of $25,000 provided ninety-nine other Chicagoans would do the same. In reporting Sharp's gesture, the Chicago *Tribune* offered its own pledge of $250. The New York Stock Exchange declared a five minute recess while its members subscribed $730 to the York fund, and Broadway producer William A. Brady arranged a benefit show. Not all contributions were so large, however. Many people contributed a dollar asking twenty-five thousand others to join them. By Christmas Eve, the campaign had met its goal with the *Banner* pledging the last $75. A grateful York wrote Edgar Foster, "I want you all to know I can never thank you enough. I thank everybody for what they have done; everyone for what they have given."[9]

His farm secure at last, York was free to turn his attention to community service and the task that he believed God had laid before him. The new landowner was particularly troubled by the poor quality of roads in Fentress County, which limited his farming to fattening cattle and hogs because of the expense of hauling crops to market. His land also included 150 acres of timber, a stand that York valued at twelve thousand dollars, but the condition of the roads made it impractical to try to haul the logs to a shipping point. Well aware that good transportation was crucial to the development of the region, York explained to a visitor from New York City, "The roads as they are separate us from the outside world. . . . There is not only timber up here but there is oil in abundance, and good roads will be to our mutual advantage." Partly due to York's prodding, by the mid-1920s, U.S. 127 was completed through the mountains and named the Alvin C. York Highway in honor of the man who had once labored with the construction gangs that built it.[10]

As much as York valued good roads, he had returned from the war convinced that education was the greatest need of the mountain people. "I ain't had much larnin' myself," York said, "so I know what an awful handicap that is." This emphasis on learning was widespread among ex-doughboys, and as a result college enrollments rose substantially in the years after World War I. York's family responsibilities precluded further schooling for him, but he was determined to give a new generation of Fentress County children the chance he had missed. The Tennessee public school system was very weak in the early 1920s, and Fentress County pupils were among the four-fifths of Tennessee children who did not have access to an elementary school with an eight-month term. Across the state, equipment was out of date or lacking entirely, and few of the teachers were college graduates. The situation was especially acute in a poor county like Fentress where one-third of school age children did not attend classes and one-fifth of the adult males were illiterate. A practical man, York was especially worried by the lack of vocational education among a people who needed marketable skills, so within a few months of his return from service, York privately resolved to build a "great non-sectarian school" in Jamestown that would provide vocational training for the young people of the county.[11]

York was certainly correct in seeing education as a great need of the mountain people, but, aside from his celebrity status, he was poorly prepared to undertake such work. He had virtually no formal education, no experience with fund raising, and no concept of how a school system should operate. He was guided in this early stage of his planning by the Alvin C. York Foundation, which featured such prominent Tennesseans as Governor Albert Roberts, Secretary of the Treasury William G. McAdoo, and Congressman Cordell Hull as members of its board of directors. An especially influential member of the board was William L. Wright, the Fentress County banker who had owned the property the Rotary Club tried to buy for York. Under the auspices of the foundation, in 1920 York began a series of lecture tours that raised twelve thousand dollars in contributions and twenty-five thousand in pledges by 1925.[12]

Although farming was his primary means of support, York personally was a rather indifferent farmer who often hired out his chores so he could devote himself to the school. Virtually a full-time fund raiser in this period, York's personal finances suffered. Even though the farm mortgage and other obligations weighed heavily on York, he often refused paying jobs in order to make the tours, accepting only enough money to pay his expenses. During the long train rides and lonely nights in distant hotel rooms, York embarked on a program of self-education by reading extensively about American history. Those who came to hear him tell of that bloody October day in the Argonne were often disappointed. "I am trying to forget the war," he told his audiences. "I occupied one space in a fifty mile front. I saw so little it hardly seems worthwhile discussing it. I'm trying to forget the war in the interest of the mountain boys and girls that I grew up among." If he could make the school a reality, York said, "I will be prouder of that than anything else I ever did."[13]

York's promotional literature for the school drew heavily on the stereotyped images of Appalachia. According to the material York and his associates circulated, the residents of Fentress County were "all white and American," people of "pure American stock" and a "Pure Pioneer strain." These hardy mountaineers had given the world Daniel Boone, Davy Crockett, Mark Twain, and even Abraham Lincoln. (The first three had at least an indirect connection with Fentress County, but Lincoln was born far to the west in Hodgenville, Kentucky.) Only a tragic lack of education kept the region from continuing to produce national leaders of similar stature. Recognizing that "Christian principles are the foundation of our government," York's proposed school would be "strictly Christian" while teaching the Bible and encouraging faith and prayer.[14]

As York's public role increased, he acquired a secretary to assist him. York freely admitted he was poorly educated, and this lack of formal schooling was often painfully evident in his correspondence. In the early 1920s, however, he made the acquaintance of a Jamestown bank official named Arthur S. Bushing, a New York native who had settled in Fentress County after marrying a local woman. Bushing became York's personal secretary and assumed most of the sergeant's writing assignments. Also a close friend and advisor, he was York's staunch ally in the long struggle to make York's mountain school a reality.[15]

York realized, of course, that raising enough money to build and operate a school was beyond his resources, so, as he had done with his road-building project, he turned to the Tennessee state government for assistance. Addressing a joint session of the General Assembly in March 1925, he called on the lawmakers to appropriate funds for a mountain school in Jamestown. Fentress County State Representative George L. Stockton immediately offered a bill to issue fifty thousand dollars in state bonds to create the Alvin C. York Agricultural Institute, but just two weeks after its introduction, the measure was narrowly defeated 41-37 in the lower chamber because, as the Nashville *Tennessean* explained, "too many members of the House had taken too firm a stand for economy to permit them to vote for another indebtedness on the state." Undeterred, Stockton quickly redrafted his proposal to require Fentress County to vote to issue seventy-five thousand dollars in bonds before it could receive a state grant of fifty thousand dollars. The modified bill passed the House 62-20 on April 9, only two days after its initial defeat. The Senate quickly followed the House's example, voting 20-10, and Governor Austin Peay signed House Bill 993 into law on April 12, 1925.[16]

Under the provisions of the new statute, the fifty thousand dollars from the state and fifty thousand from Fentress County would go toward building, equipping, and operating the York Agricultural Institute. To this sum would be added the money York had secured in his fund-raising efforts. The other twenty-five thousand dollars from the Fentress County bonds would go into the construction of an elementary school. To oversee these efforts, the act created a Board of Trust to take charge of the money, select a site, and begin construction. The measure named York chairman of the board, with banker W.L. Wright, county school superintendent O.O. Frogge, attorney J.T. Wheeler, farmer James Linder, Max Colditz, and W.M. Johnson as members. After the board had completed the school, it was to turn the institute over to the State Board of Education which would operate it.[17]

Almost immediately, York found himself in the midst of a bitter struggle with his fellow board members over school policy. Administration of the schools was an important component of political power in the mountains because the location of a school could influence property values, and teaching positions were plums in a region where jobs were scarce. Traditionally, control of the schools rested with establishment figures such as Wright and Frogge; York represented a challenge to their customary monopoly in such matters. A person of little education, moderate means, and no social position, he would have been an insignificant man in Fentress County had it not been for the renown his heroism had brought; yet York insisted the board accept his leadership in virtually all matters. True believer that he was, York refused to compromise any of his plans for the school to suit the county elite.[18]

The main issue dividing the members of the Board of Trust was the selection of a building site. As a resident of Pall Mall in the northern part of the county, York favored a location on U.S. 127 roughly a mile north of the courthouse in Jamestown, but County Superintendent O.O. Frogge preferred another site south of town. York charged that Frogge preferred the southern tract because its proximity to homes owned by justices of the peace would enhance the value of their property and thus nurture Frogge's political clout. As York explained matters to Governor Austin Peay, he was "Doing All I can to git this school located. And I will say that I am almost having to git my location Single-Handed," because certain members of the board have a "Personal Interest in the South Town Site." When the two sides proved unable to compromise, York angrily resigned from the board in March 1926 and announced his intention to establish the York Industrial School. With the money he had raised from lecturing, he held a "Dirt-Breaking" on the northern site on May 8 with some two thousand people looking on.[19]

York's independent course created new problems for him because the legislature had specified the school would be an agricultural institute and had placed one hundred thousand dollars in state and local funds under the control of the Board of Trust. Consequently, York could neither use the money without the approval of the Board of Trust nor could he use it to build an "industrial" institute, obstacles he surmounted by returning to the General Assembly in 1927 and securing a change in the law. Once again addressing a joint session, York declared that so little progress had been made on the school that he was embarrassed to talk about it. Without mentioning names, he blamed political infighting for the delays and urged the legislators to amend the 1925 act by setting aside the existing Board of Trust and vesting its authority in the State Board of Education. The lawmakers complied on April 1, naming York, as well as the regular members of the state board, a trustee. The sergeant then dropped his plans for a separate "industrial" school.[20]

The state board quickly approved the northern site, but between 1927 and 1929, the construction of the school proceeded against the backdrop of angry squabbling over York's relationship to the school. Several prominent Fentress Countians, including two members of the old Board of Trust, peti-

tioned the State Board of Education to prevent York from being "elected or employed . . . as the head or in any way in the
control or management" of the school. Alleging that York
planned to use the school to teach his religious beliefs, they
charged that his leadership "would greatly injure the school,
impede its progress and be against the best interest of the people." The signers included Wright and Frogge as well as the
county judge, the county court clerk, the county tax assessor,
the chairman of the local board of education, the coroner, and
the sheriff. York's attorney, W.A. Garrett, countered that the
opponents of his client had "refused absolutely to cooperate
with Sgt. York in any particular" but instead sought to use
York "merely as a 'figurehead'" and "take all the honor for
promoting and making the school possible away from him
and take the honor and praise unto themselves." Garrett and
York accused the county board of education of seeking "more
power, money, and prestige" and derided Frogge as a "small
sized, little County politician and grafter" seeking "to perpetuate himself in office as County Superintendent. . . . "21

Arthur Bushing became a particular target for York's opponents in this increasingly bitter confrontation. People who
were unwilling to assail York personally could direct their
ire toward the sergeant's secretary. Bushing's New York City
origins made him particularly vulnerable to criticism in the
rather parochial atmosphere of Fentress County. For example, in a vicious personal attack, a local editor derided Bushing
as "obnoxious to all right-thinking people," and the
"troublemaker of this county." He labeled Bushing a "vin-
dictive writer" and claimed "it would be hard to find a prominent citizen of this county you haven't puked all over." While
denying he was "attacking the noble sergeant," the editor
pointedly called on York to "fire his secretary, and hire one
of our boys—if he needs one."22

Finally, in late 1927, York lashed out at his enemies in a
series of lawsuits. He sued a neighbor over a boundary question involving a spring; he sued the Jamestown Light Company over its use of a building on some property he owned;
and he filed ouster petitions against County Superintendent

Frogge and members of the county school board. Frogge was also included in a suit York initiated on September 16 "in behalf of all school children of Fentress County," asking seven hundred fifty thousand dollars in damages against ten Fentress County men who supposedly had "hampered him and his co-workers and annoyed him and caused him to suffer much humiliation and mental pain and anguish." Besides Frogge, the suit included three other former trustees, State Representative Stockton, the county judge, and a county trustee, all of whom, York said, had obstructed his efforts to build the school.[23]

York's excellent political connections in Nashville were immensely beneficial to him in his battles with local rivals. Throughout the 1920s, Tennessee's Democratic party divided roughly along a rural-urban axis, especially in gubernatorial races. In 1922, the rural faction took power with the election of Austin Peay to the governor's chair, and it remained in control for the next ten years. A prime example of the "business progressives" who were elected to governorships in many southern states during the twenties, Peay was a lawyer, farmer, and businessman anxious to improve the efficiency of state government and to upgrade public services. He particularly catered to rural Tennesseans by using state money to build roads and schools for areas like Fentress County that were too poor themselves to provide such services adequately. Thus Peay's program for the state as a whole meshed neatly with York's goals for the mountains. Already a partisan Democrat, York became a strong backer of Austin Peay and the rural faction in Republican Fentress County.[24]

York's ties with the rural faction were further enhanced by his links with a close Peay associate, Colonel Luke Lea. The descendant of a family long prominent in Tennessee affairs, Lea had a meteoric rise in politics, winning election to the senate in 1911 when he was barely thirty. Although he was defeated in his bid for reelection in 1916, Lea restored much of the glamour to his name with a brief yet dramatic military career during World War I. He organized the all-volunteer 114th Field Artillery Regiment and served ably as its colonel in France, but his most spectacular exploit came after the Armistice was signed when he and a small group of men entered neutral Holland and bluffed their way into the castle housing the abdicated emperor, Kaiser Wilhelm II of Germany. Their avowed purpose was to kidnap the monarch and present him as a New Year's gift to President Wilson in Paris. While the scheme was thwarted, it enhanced Lea's already respectable service record, and he returned to Tennessee a hero. Although he never again sought elective office, Lea became a powerful figure in the twenties by placing his wealth, his contacts, and his newspaper, the Nashville *Tennessean*, at the service of candidates whom he favored, among them Austin Peay.[25]

Despite their obvious differences, the Nashville aristocrat and the Pall Mall farmer had much in common. Both had served with distinction in the war, were enthusiastic members of the American Legion, and were interested in bringing roads and schools to Tennessee. Moreover, Lea and York each had something to offer the other. Lea's political connections could help York against his local opponents while the *Tennessean* could provide publicity to expedite fund-raising efforts. In this connection, for example, Lea and Peay arranged meetings for York with several important newspaper publishers and sent a *Tennessean* reporter to prepare a story on the York Institute for the *New York Times*. For his part, York's popularity and reputation for integrity boosted the stature of the rural faction of the Democratic party in predominantly Republican East Tennessee.[26]

York was most active in the gubernatorial primaries of 1926 and 1928, contests that featured major challenges to the rural faction and also coincided with the period of most intense controversy over the school. In 1926, York worked hard for Peay in Fentress County, stressing the governor's road program and his "educational accomplishment." Fully two months before the primary, York wrote to Peay to assure him that " . . . we are scotching all the lies we hear, and working hard from now on for your re-election." In spite of York's efforts, the county establishment swung Fentress to Peay's

opponent, State Treasurer Hill McAlister, with 52 percent of
the vote, even though Peay was very popular in the rest of
the Tennessee mountains and carried East Tennessee as a
whole with 68 percent. In the fall election against Republican
Walter White, Peay made political history in Tennessee by
becoming the first Democrat since the Civil War to win East
Tennessee from a Republican opponent, but he again lost in
Fentress County, where White took 57 percent of the vote
compared with 47 percent in East Tennessee and 35 percent
in the state as a whole. Clearly the county political organization was strongly opposed to York and his friends.[27]

York played an even more visible and important role in
the tumultuous 1928 primary. Austin Peay died on October
2, 1927, and Speaker of the Senate Henry Horton succeeded
him as governor. The sixty-one-year old Marshall County
farmer was a man of limited political experience, so he came
to rely heavily on the powerful Lea for guidance. Through the
boom period of the late twenties, Lea was closely associated
with Nashville businessman Rogers Caldwell, the founder of
a pioneer conglomerate named Caldwell and Company.
Shortly after Horton took office, charges began to circulate
that Lea and Caldwell were manipulating the naive governor
for their personal profit. The Nashville *Banner*, published by
Lea's personal enemy and business rival E.B. Stahlman, gave
these accusations a great deal of attention and helped to make
them the focal point of the 1928 gubernatorial primary, involving Horton, McAllister, and attorney Lewis Pope.[28]

Alvin York's testimony was an important part of the
defense the Lea-Horton faction constructed against such at-
tacks. In the last days of the campaign the sergeant joined
Lea and Horton in a public statement upholding the integrity of the governor and his associates while excoriating
York's former benefactor Stahlman who, York said, hated Colonel Lea because the German-born *Banner* publisher had been
"pro-German" during the war. Furthermore, York accused
Stahlman of trying to have Lea dismissed from his regiment
before the outfit sailed for France in order to make him appear cowardly. Failing in that, Stahlman then tried to have

Lea court-martialed after the kaiser episode in Holland. Stahlman opposed Lea, York declared, because of "newspaper competition" and his "failure to make Lea bend to his will." York's denunciation of Stahlman was apparently related to the long wrangle over the farm payments. Acutely embarrassed by the affair, York had blamed Stahlman and the *Banner* for placing him in an awkward situation by giving him a farm he had never requested and then expecting him to pay for it. Stung by the attack, Stahlman denied everything, declaring that he had been an American citizen "long before Luke Lea saw light of day." Stahlman rebuked York more gently, calling him a "child of the hills, with heart as trustful and unsuspicious as it is brave and upright," who "became easy prey of designing counselors."[29]

Despite Stahlman's denials, the York statement helped to shore up the faltering Horton who narrowly defeated McAlister and Pope, 45 percent to 43 percent to 12 percent, respectively. In Fentress County, opposition to York's political associates remained strong. Horton won 44 percent of the vote, virtually the same percentage won by Austin Peay two years earlier, but the candidacy of Lewis Pope, a product of nearby Bledsoe County, split the anti-rural faction tally with Pope taking 31 percent and McAlister 22 percent. Horton won the general election against Republican Raleigh Hopkins 61 percent to 39 percent, but Fentress County gave him only 35 percent as opposed to 46 percent throughout East Tennessee.[30]

York had stood by Lea and Horton in a difficult time, and he soon claimed his reward. In mid-1928, State Commissioner of Education Perry L. Harned authorized York to accept applications for teaching positions in the name of the board. To York's dismay, however, his recommendation for elementary school principal was subsequently rejected by the board in favor of a candidate supported by O.O. Frogge. The outraged York protested to Governor Horton, "My wishes in this regard have been ruthlessly set aside, and your enemies and mine allowed to dominate, over my protest." Describing himself as "deeply humiliated," York declared, "I have already made great sacrifices and will continue to do so, but only on the condition that I cease to be cuffed and kicked about and made to appear ridiculous at the instance of men who are enemies of all true progress, hence likewise your opponents also." Replying for the governor, Harned wrote, "I regret more than I can express the existing differences," but politely insisted that the law gave the state board final responsibility for choosing personnel.[31]

Still determined that "some small consideration should be accorded me in determining policy and administration," York escalated his demands for a role in running the school as the time for the formal opening of the York Agricultural Institute grew closer. York personally preferred the creation of a new board of trustees with himself as chairman to assume complete control. Otherwise, he wanted "my name . . . given back to me for uses which I shall have for same in a similar educational program elsewhere." Clearly York could not be given personal control of an institution built with public funds, so Luke Lea suggested that York be named president and business manager of the school, in effect empowered to act as the agent of the board of education. Lea's close friend Thomas Henderson, an important figure in the Tennessee Democratic party, worked out the details with those involved, and on August 10, 1929, the state board voted to place the newly completed structure under York's management. The move delighted York and satisfied the friends of the rural faction in Fentress County, one of whom wrote Governor Horton that "every true Horton supporter in this county approves of what you have done. Of course the Anti-Administration and Anti-York faction think you have erred."[32]

The new president was barely installed before he faced his first major crisis. With the 1929-30 term about to open, York's enemies now argued that the law creating the school obligated the state rather than Fentress County to fund the York Institute, and under the leadership of County Judge H.N. Wright, a York opponent, the county court refused to vote money to operate the school. The state board also balked at releasing funds, so the court sued the board in mid-October,

and on December 2, the Tennessee Supreme Court ruled that
the law required the state to finance the York Institute, a decision Wright said meant "a great saving to the taxpayers of
the county." The case decided, school opened immediately
with state support, making Alvin York's ten-year dream a
reality.[33]

The York Institute held its first classes one month after
the stock market crash ushered in America's greatest depression. As president and business manager of a fledgling school,
York was hard-pressed to keep his project afloat during those
difficult years, especially when the state began reducing its
support in the face of declining revenues. Simultaneously,
York's friends Lea and Horton were implicated in a major
scandal, and their faction of the Democratic party was beaten
at the polls in 1932. With his influence diminishing, York
suffered an important setback in 1931 when the state board
stopped supplying money for bus transportation, an item
crucial to a school in a rural district. He turned to the county
court for funds, but George Stockton and W.L. Wright successfully opposed the move, citing an opinion by state Attorney General L.D. Smith based on the 1929 Supreme Court
ruling that the state must provide the money for all institute
operations. Rather than lose the buses, York decided to pay
for them out of his own pocket. By mortgaging his farm, he
scraped together enough money to buy and service buses and
hire drivers. His action shows the depth of his commitment,
but the mortgage placed a severe strain on the York family
throughout the depression-ridden thirties. Asked later about
those difficult years, Gracie York often said she preferred not
to discuss that time, although she confided to a son-in-law
that she would never again permit the property to be mortgaged.[34]

York's burden was increased by his spontaneous generos-
ity and his willingness to assist other members of his family.
Any guest in his home was welcome to stay for dinner, and
Mrs. York often had to set the large dining room table two
or three times to accommodate all of her husband's callers.
When the son of his longtime personal secretary Arthur S.

Bushing started to college, York loaned Arthur, Jr., money for
his freshman year. When York's mother became so infirm she
could no longer stay alone, she came to live with Alvin until
her death some ten years later in 1945. During that period,
York bore the expense of her care and paid the funeral costs
after her death. In addition, he loaned money to relatives and
cosigned notes for them, occasionally finding his confidence
betrayed. Commenting on the sergeant's financial plight, a
York acquaintance explained, "He might get along if he didn't
keep helping his kinfolks out so much."[35]

By the late 1930s, York's finances were so strained that
Senator Thomas Stewart introduced a bill to give York the
rank and retired pay of a colonel in order to ease his plight.
Similar proposals had been introduced intermittently since
1919 by Congressman Hull and Senator McKellar but none
had received legislative approval, at least partly because the
army feared such action would establish a troublesome prece-
dent. Stewart sought to overcome this obstacle by appealing
to Franklin Roosevelt, explaining that York was "improvident" and had "almost run through the farm that was given
him." York will "starve to death," Stewart warned FDR, "if
the Government doesn't take care of him." Roosevelt declined
to lobby for the bill but his secretary, General Edwin "Pa"
Watson, assured Stewart, "it will be given very sympathetic
attention when it arrives here." Without Roosevelt's active
support, however, the measure quietly died.[36]

Probably York's most bitter disappointment of those hard
years was his ouster as president of the York Institute.
Although York's commitment to the school ran very deep,
his own lack of formal education handicapped him as an administrator, and his enemies in Fentress County were highly
critical of his leadership. Moreover, some professional
educators had long been doubtful of York's ability to provide
effective management for the school. Admitting "there is a
need for better schools in the community in which Sergeant
Alvin York lives," President Bruce R. Payne of George Peabody College for Teachers and a former member of the York
School Foundation Board voiced the skepticism of many

when he said, "York has a good deal of determination, but he has no education himself. He is consecrated to the idea but it takes more than consecration to do these things."[37]

In October 1933, a special committee of the State Board of Education visited Jamestown to investigate the situation at the school, and their detailed report to the board's executive committee dealt harshly with York's direction of the institute. After listing what it considered to be instances of waste and mismanagement, the committee concluded that "the vast amount of money heretofore appropriated has, to a very large extent, been wasted, insofar as real accomplishments of the purposes for which the taxpayers have been required to donate. This gross waste is little short of criminal extravagance." Beyond these matters, the committee continued, "our impression is that this school has no 'punch.'" It found "no vision on the part of anyone connected with the school, and the work that is being attempted is very poor." Of York personally the committee said, "We seriously doubt his ability to head an educational institution with any degree of success."[38]

York replied to the charges in a report submitted to the board and Governor Hill McAlister. He rejected the findings of the committee as "quite unfair, and at variance with the real facts," indicating, for example, that what the committee had called a "junk room" could just as easily have been described as storage space. Conceding that "the school is falling far short of its opportunity to serve the real and practical needs of the section," York insisted that the board must bear a share of the blame because it had final responsibility for the institute. He deplored the "quite unjustifiable criticism of myself as President of the Institute" and said that his job had been greatly complicated by "outside, outraged citizen interference."[39]

The board was understandably reluctant to take formal action against York, but in the summer of 1935 the situation at the school became even worse when York asked the board to dismiss principal Henry Clay Brier for what York labeled his "moral conduct," saying only that charges had been filed with him by "citizens and students all of which I have thoroughly investigated and am convinced there is [sic] sufficient grounds for immediate dismissal." While York refused to elaborate, Brier's friends charged that the president was angry over Brier's refusal to give a larger raise to his brother Jim York, a janitor at the school. When the board refused to fire Brier, York announced he would not serve as president, so board member Robert L. Forrester took over the administration of the York Institute for the 1935-36 term. The climax of the dispute came at a meeting of the state board on May 8, 1936. His effectiveness destroyed, Brier submitted his resignation, but the board accorded him a vote of confidence and then acted to combine the jobs of business manager and principal, giving York the title of president emeritus.[40]

The bureaucratic sleight of hand ended York's direct control over the school that bore his name. He contemptuously spurned the title of president emeritus "since I am not yet ready to retire and join the company of the superannuated," and compared himself to "the late Cal Coolidge," saying, "I do not choose to run" for president emeritus. "It's my school. I founded it and built it," he declared, threatening to ask the next state legislature to turn it over to him. When the board named a new principal, Paul B. Stephens, York warned that "he is going to take orders from me." Despite his bluster, however, York stepped quietly aside when Stephens arrived to assume his duties.[41]

Although his legal connection with the school was now severed, York retained a lively interest in its affairs and continued to contribute substantial sums of money to its projects. In late 1937, the National Youth Administration and the Works Progress Administration offered to do some construction work for the institute if it would supply some three thousand dollars in raw materials. Even more important than the new industrial arts and recreation building for the school, the project would also provide a number of jobs for unemployed workers in Fentress County. Well aware that three thousand dollars was a considerable sum for Tennessee's tight budget, Congressman Albert Hogue wrote Governor Gordon Browning, "This work is more important than a balanced budget to this section. . . . Please help us." Despite his own financial problems, York stepped in to offer fifteen hundred dollars for the work if the state would provide the additional fifteen hundred. Nashville officials had initially refused the request for three thousand dollars, but after York's action Browning and Acting Budget Director Henry Burke provided the needed money.[42]

Ironically, York's generosity set the stage for his last major dispute with school officials. Roughly a year and a half after the state released the fifteen hundred dollars, York charged Stephens with the misuse of NYA funds in a letter to Governor Prentice Cooper. Demanding Stephen's dismissal, York accused him of using state gasoline and oil in his personal car, paying a man who had done work for him with a drum of state-owned gasoline, diverting money from the school construction fund to buy hogs for himself, and withholding money from student workers. This latest clash over the school deeply irritated the members of the state board, especially after a special inquiry found the charges "groundless." One official complained that "investigations at the school have become a semi-annual affair," and a member of the board resigned in disgust over the wrangling. Nevertheless, on October 10, 1939, Stephens was transferred to the Division of Vocational Rehabilitation, and C.W. Davis replaced him as business manager and principal. Like Brier, Stephens had been removed in order to restore peace at the York Institute, although the board expressed its confidence in both men.[43]

The Stephens ouster ended York's real influence with the state board. His leadership had proven erratic and sometimes disruptive, so the board became less willing to hear his views. As one member expressed it to York, "It is not good diplomacy to let a man be head of a school who hasn't a college degree." For his part, York grew more concerned with religious education, preparedness work, and oil prospecting, activities that reduced the amount of time he had for the York Institute.

Nevertheless, York and the school remained closely identified with each other in the popular mind, and the sergeant considered its construction to be his greatest achievement.[44]

York's postwar career brought real accomplishments but it was also marked by a great deal of failure and disappointment. He nearly lost his farm in 1921, and the place was deeply mortgaged in the 1930s to finance school buses for the York Institute, a remarkable personal sacrifice that clouded York's financial future for years. The harshest blow, however, was his ouster as president and business manager of the school that bore his name. The long battle over the school illustrates York's strengths and weaknesses as a public figure in the years after World War I. A man of honesty and integrity, he was convinced that education was important for mountain children, and he was determined to build a school in Jamestown. Playing on his notoriety, he was able to marshal resources for his project that would have been unavailable to anyone else in his region. Unfortunately, however, York did not recognize the limits of his talents and insisted on controlling every aspect of the school's operation even though he lacked the training or experience for the task. The righteous soldier of the Lord who had scourged the Germans in the Argonne did not have the flexibility essential to the management of a public institution like a school. But whatever his failings as an administrator, York had still performed a fine service against difficult odds. Motivated by a religious-based sense of obligation to his community, he had translated his popular renown into a lasting contribution to the lives of his neighbors.

6. The Legend Makers

Despite Alvin York's relative obscurity during the 1920s and 1930s, he still held a place in the popular imagination. Under contract to a New York booking agency, he did well on the lecture circuit talking about mountain life and promoting the school. Writers who advocated patriotic, religious, or educational causes did occasional newspaper and magazine pieces about him that brought readers up to date on his activities. In addition, books about York's life published by major presses appeared in 1922, 1928, and 1930. Most important in establishing York as a permanent part of American lore, however, was the highly successful 1941 film *Sergeant York* which dramatically packaged his story for a mass audience on the eve of World War II. The cumulative effect of all this was to perpetuate and expand the York legend as originally set forth by George Pattullo in his *Saturday Evening Post* article.

The legend-making process had an enormous impact on Alvin York. The books and the movie often sacrificed the truth about him to their effort to make him a symbol of certain national values. The reality of the man faded behind the public image and the sergeant assumed the stressful role of trying to live up to the expectations of others. At the same time, however, York demonstrated a certain skill at turning publicity to the service of causes he espoused. For Alvin York, becoming a hero was another unpleasant task he performed because he believed his patriotic duty demanded it.

Important to the creation of the York legend was the

writing done first by Samuel K. Cowan and later by Thomas Skeyhill, the authors of the three biographies. All three books are similar, noncritical accounts of York's life to 1919 based on interviews with Fentress Countians, members of the York family, and the sergeant himself. Because of the personal contacts Cowan and Skeyhill made, their books are important sources of information about York's obscure early life, but the authors were primarily concerned with portraying their subject as a man of truly epic proportions. Using biographical data to develop the themes put forward by Pattullo, they offered the public an archetypical American frontiersman called to be a soldier of the Lord in the war to end all wars. In the process, Cowan and Skeyhill distorted the reality of York's existence and used the popular stereotypes of Appalachia to obscure rather than explain the patterns of his life.

In 1921, freelance journalist Samuel K. Cowan arrived in Pall Mall to begin collecting material about York. A native Tennessean himself, Cowan was born in Nashville in 1869 and started his career there as a newspaper reporter in the 1890s. He left the newspaper business to freelance in 1914 and contributed pieces to *Literary Digest*, *Mentor*, and *McClure's*, among others, until he joined the *Literary Digest* as an editor eight years later. York was a logical topic for a writer with Tennessee connections, and the sergeant proved to be cooperative, granting Cowan interviews and showing him portions of his private diary.[1]

Cowan's stay in Fentress County resulted in *Sergeant York and His People*, published by Funk and Wagnalls in 1922. The book purported to set York against the backdrop of his mountain heritage and thereby explain how so allegedly unusual a figure could appear in the midst of a contemporary industrial society. Tracing York's lineage back to his great-great-grandfather Conrad Pile, Cowan reiterated the popular belief that the isolation of the Cumberland Mountains had preserved the pioneer virtues that in turn had shaped Alvin York. Accepting the common view that Appalachian people were twentieth-century pioneers who had sprung directly from Elizabethan England, Cowan considered them the "purest Anglo-

Saxons to be found today," a people who are "Colonial-Americans in their speech and cadences." He spiced his account with a great deal of local color but really told surprisingly little about York himself. Despite his lyric descriptions of the inhabitants of Pall Mall and the surrounding countryside, Cowan said virtually nothing about York before the war, nor did he discuss his life after the Armistice. In short, *Sergeant York and His People* is really a patriotic tract which offers no substantial analysis of Alvin York or his Appalachian neighbors. Although it received only tepid reviews and had limited circulation, Cowan's book has proven to be rather durable. Grosset and Dunlap reissued it during World War II, and more recently a Fentress County organization has printed a new edition to raise money for a proposed Alvin York Museum in Jamestown.[2]

A few years after Cowan's visit, Thomas Skeyhill approached York about doing another book based on the sergeant's war diary. Much closer to York's age than Cowan, Skeyhill was an Oxford-educated Australian who had served as a signaler in the Eighth Australian Infantry during the war. A twice-wounded combat veteran, Skeyhill was blinded by a shell explosion during the Gallipoli campaign; an operation restored his sight. During 1918 he toured the United States as part of the third Liberty Loan drive and decided to make this country his home even though he remained an Australian citizen. Skeyhill first glimpsed York during the latter's tour of New York in 1919 and was deeply impressed by the man and his story. While driving through Tennessee in the spring of 1927, he yielded to a sudden impulse to pay York a call. "I had no thought at that time of writing with him his story," Skeyhill declared. "I just wanted to satisfy a personal urge." Whatever actually prompted Skeyhill's considerable detour, the two veterans quickly became close friends, and Skeyhill returned to Pall Mall for an extended visit.[3]

Aware of the possiblities inherent in the York story, Skeyhill gingerly broached the subject of a book. Skeyhill's timing was fortuitous. Beyond his plans for the school, York also had substantial personal obligations that left him hard-pressed for money. At one point during the fight over the school, York had contacted a publisher about his war diary. Because the diary itself was brief and sketchy, the firm had suggested that York supplement it with a full account of his life. At first York had agreed, then later changed his mind and dropped the project. Now Skeyhill revived the idea, urging York to collaborate with him on an "autobiography." The sergeant refused, suggesting that Skeyhill write his own book, but the latter insisted on York's participation. He told York he had a patriotic duty to share his story with the American people who had honored him so richly. Moreover, the publicity would greatly benefit his still-struggling school. York pondered the matter again and a week later took the diary from his bank strongbox and placed it at Skeyhill's disposal. "Jes tell the truth," Skeyhill quoted York as saying, "the whole truth, and let it go at that."[4]

Skeyhill set to work eagerly. He researched the records of the War Department pertaining to the incident in the Argonne and tracked down several of York's fellow soldiers to interview them about the firefight. Perhaps most important, he made himself at home in the Valley of the Three Forks of the Wolf where he became popular with the residents. The children adopted him as their playmate, and even the shy Gracie York relaxed in his company. Within a year, Skeyhill produced a manuscript, purportedly in York's own words, that presented a thin narrative of his life flavored with picturesque vignettes of mountain life. *Sergeant York: His Own Life Story and War Diary* appeared in 1928, and two years later Skeyhill published a rewritten version for school children under the title *Sergeant York: Last of the Long Hunters*.[5]

The books by Cowan and Skeyhill have deeply influenced public perceptions of York. The scriptwriters for the film *Sergeant York* drew heavily on their work as have most journalists who have written about York in any depth. In their hands, York emerged as the "typical" mountaineer, a "pure" Anglo-Saxon who spoke in old English dialect and worshipped the harsh Jehovah of the Old Testament. An unsophisticated child of nature, York lived by his wits and his intuition. He foreswore the rewards of industrial society, preferring the company of his dogs and his rifle. When the real York did not quite fit the mold, Cowan and Skeyhill simply modified the truth. For example, Skeyhill wrote most of the autobiography as if York himself were telling the story in first person. Although Skeyhill had York speak in mountain dialect, people who knew both the writer and his subject contend that Skeyhill gave York an accent he did not really have. Indeed, Skeyhill admitted as much when he acknowledged that years of contact with the outside world had modified the sergeant's speech pattern.[6]

The York presented by both writers is a one-dimensional, prefabricated character whose real essence has been sacrificed to the mythmaking process. Cowan and Skeyhill made York an attractive but unbelievable person who simply has no faults worth mentioning. The depth and complexity of the man have been sacrificed to the effort to make him inspirational. As a result, the authors missed the truly engaging part of the York story, namely, the struggle of a very average person to manage an unwanted celebrity status that changed his life. Being a hero placed York in an awkward position. While pressures on him increased and people demanded much more of him, his new stature did not bring a corresponding increase in his ability to handle such pressure. He was no better educated or appreciably richer after the war than before, yet his life had become much more difficult. Struggling to rationalize and order his personal circumstances, the real York was much more inspirational than the statuelike figure described by Cowan and Skeyhill.

Given their noncritical approach, Cowan and Skeyhill failed to examine a number of apparent contradictions between the legendary York and the flesh-and-blood man. Indeed the mere existence of these books seems to challenge their claims that York did not really want his story published. Cowan and Skeyhill repeatedly stressed York's modesty and his reluctance to discuss the fight in the Argonne, especially for commercial purposes. Skeyhill in particular gave a rather lengthy account of his efforts to coax an unwilling York into cooperating with him. Yet by 1930 York had participated in the writing of three books and had made one overture to a publisher himself: hardly the record of a man determined to avoid the limelight. In fact York had good reason to understand the value of favorable publicity as well as anyone, and he certainly realized its importance to his efforts in education. Such shrewdness is not compatible with the authors' ideal of an innocent child of nature, so Cowan and Skeyhill simply ignored the point.[7]

Cowan and Skeyhill were equally unwilling to confront York's financial problems. They emphasized York's indifference to material gain, even though throughout his life either York himself or others acting in his name repeatedly sought contributions for projects connected with him. At the time Cowan and Skeyhill were writing, York lived on a farm purchased by public subscription and was building a school in part through public donations. In the late 1930s, he launched another drive to build a Bible school in Fentress County, and years later still another fund drive mounted by others raised the money to pay his delinquent taxes shortly before his death. While Cowan and Skeyhill were certainly correct in saying that York was not personally greedy, nevertheless, his personal circumstances and his plans for the mountains prompted him to solicit money repeatedly. For much of the 1920s, York was virtually a full-time fund raiser as he worked to get the York Institute started. Significantly, York's financial problems never became a part of his public image, nor was he ever described in print as a "typical" indigent mountaineer who was unable to handle money. This unheroic aspect of his life was simply ignored.

Another contradiction overlooked by the mythmakers concerns York's attitude toward his homeland. They described his rural life as pastoral and idyllic. Strengthened by physical labor and nurtured by maternal love, York faced the vicissitudes of life with a noble grace. Such an interpretation contrasts sharply with the harshness of turn-of-the-century life in Fentress County, Tennessee. The authors rendered York's poverty picturesque, even character building. His lack of formal education became a virtue worthy of respect. Like many middle-aged men, the York of the 1920's felt a certain nostalgia for the world of his youth, although such nostalgia never erased his memories of early hardships. Far from working to preserve an agrarian Appalachia, York struggled to bring industrialization and modernization to the mountains, but the irony of this escaped his biographers. They praised York as a child of nature who spontaneously did the right thing, while they simultaneously applauded his efforts to secure formal education for Appalachian children. York's agrarian existence allegedly made him one of nature's noblemen, yet future generations of Fentress Countians should learn a trade at the York Agricultural Institute and drive to their factory jobs on the Alvin C. York Highway.

Perhaps most importantly, Cowan and Skeyhill failed to analyze the fundamental contradiction of York's life, that of the violent Christian. Despite the fact that the sergeant's religious faith is central to his legend, his chroniclers offered little real discussion of his beliefs. The Church of Christ in Christian Union was a fundamentalist group, but both Skeyhill and Cowan avoided that term, probably because fundamentalism was controversial in the 1920s. Indeed Skeyhill's York carefully sidestepped the celebrated Scopes trial held in Dayton, Tennessee. "I ain't a-going to argue nohow about this here evolution," York commented. The sergeant had his own beliefs, and "I ain't a-going to change them for any trial at Dayton or anywhere else." However, neither Cowan nor Skeyhill ever discussed what those beliefs might be. By taking such a vague and bland approach, they guaranteed that no one would be offended by York's particular brand of Christianity, and also enabled the reader to project his own beliefs onto the sergeant.[8]

Moreover, Cowan and Skeyhill offered very little real evidence that salvation had changed York's life in any important way. According to their accounts, religion led York away from smoking, drinking, cardplaying, and cursing but really affected little else about him. Always a churchgoer, always a hard worker, always a devoted family man, York's conversion apparently did no more than modify a few personal habits. The one radical change religion brought to his life — pacifism — he quickly abandoned for the more comfortable role of Christian warrior. While York's faith was certainly sincere, its roots seem to have been more cultural than spiritual. Consequently, he often saw the hand of God in decisions that were perhaps shaped more by the environment that produced him. For example, in deciding to accept combat duty, York was following the lead of his ancestors and his neighbors. His own taste for violence was already clear. Assuming the posture of a soldier of the Lord simply gave York a theological justification for a course of action that the logic of his heritage virtually dictated to him. Pall Mall might produce heroes or scoundrels, but not pacifists.

Given the contradictory nature of their interpretations, Skeyhill and Cowan came eventually to an untenable conclusion about York, namely, that he was somehow both a unique and a representative American, the product of an agrarian society that had to be destroyed to make way for the brighter future industrialization would surely bring to the mountains. Presumably the values that produced Sergeant York would also be swept away in the process, but Skeyhill and Cowan found York's true greatness to rest in his determination to facilitate Appalachia's transition to the industrial age. In short, they praised York for working to create a society that would not produce the kind of man they believed Alvin York to be. As a result, Skeyhill and Cowan unwittingly made York into a symbol of American decline, a living reminder of greatness irretrievably lost with the passing of the frontier.

Eleven years after Skeyhill's second book appeared, Warner Brothers studio released the motion picture *Sergeant York*. Dramatic and entertaining, it was an instant commercial success and virtually guaranteed York's enduring fame. While the filmmakers drew on the writings of Cowan and Skeyhill in preparing the script, they presented York in a slightly different context. *Sergeant York* is part of a tradition of Depression era films such as *The Grapes of Wrath, Meet John Doe,* and *Mr. Deeds Goes to Town*, which affirmed the wisdom and decency of the common man in the face of adversity. The "reel" Alvin York was an unambiguous metaphor for patriotism at a time of intense national crisis. York's allegedly unique Appalachian heritage was important in the film, but the emphasis was clearly on his difficult decision to fight for his country, a decision similar to the ones many Americans were facing in the months before Pearl Harbor. Far from symbolizing a lost America, the film York called up images of American righteousness, a sense of battling evil in the name of justice. The books about Sergeant York told the story of an anachronism and quickly went out of print, but the film presented a man wrestling with a timeless moral dilemma and has become a cinema classic.

York's decision to permit the filming of his life grew out of yet another contradiction in his life, namely, his simultaneous commitment to both isolation and preparedness. By the mid 1930s, York's attitude toward World War I and warfare in general had changed substantially since 1919. Discussing the Great War with a visitor, York concluded, "I can't see that we did any good. There's as much trouble now as there was when we were over there. I think the slogan of 'A war to end war,' is all wrong." Now implicitly rejecting the view that America had fought God's battle in the struggle, York clearly shared the disillusionment felt by many Americans regarding United States participation in the Great War, and his views reflected the popular drift toward isolationism. "I would fight again," he said, "but I would not volunteer unless the trouble came to America. Of course, then I'd volunteer, but never to fight oversees[sic]." In the future the United States should let "those fellows fight their own battles and we'll fight ours when the time comes."[9]

However, York's isolationism was balanced by his commitment to preparedness. Asked in 1934 whether arming or disarming was the surest road to peace, York replied, "That's getting in deep water. Disarmament would do it if everybody would disarm but everybody won't. I'm strong for preparedness. I think the better equipped we are along military lines the less chance we have of getting into a war with some other nation." Responding to the Japanese attack on China in 1937, York warned, "Japan is fighting an undeclared war in China and after it conquers that country it is going to come over here. I'd just as soon we got into it now as later." As for Nazi Germany, he counseled, "I believe if we want to stop Hitler we must knock him off the block."[10]

Just as York's contradictory feelings about World War I had reflected the nation's ambivalence about that earlier conflict, so his blend of isolationism and preparedness in the late 1930s captured the national mood and made him prominent once more. As events in Europe and Asia grew increasingly ominous, Americans began to reevaluate their nation's involvement in the Great War of twenty years before. With the rise of Nazi Germany, the idea that the United States had been duped or manipulated into a needless foreign adventure was tempered by the feeling that there were indeed evil forces in the world and that America must meet the challenge they presented. This changing climate of opinion fostered a renewed interest in the story of American's reluctant doughboy whose hard choice between peace and justice in 1917 suddenly seemed so pertinent to the decisions facing the entire nation.

One of the first to recognize the timeliness of the York story was Jesse L. Lasky, a Hollywood motion picture producer fallen on hard times. The son of a San Francisco shoeseller, Lasky had started in show business as a cornet player with a traveling medicine show but rose to head his own motion piture company, Famous Players-Lasky, which later became the core of Paramount Pictures. Forced out of the company he had helped found during an executive shakeup in 1932, he was left nearly bankrupt due to a collapse in Paramount stock. After three years with Twentieth Century Fox and three more with Pickford-Lasky Corporation, he was reduced to producing radio shows when the latter folded in 1938. Lasky had wanted to do a film about Alvin York ever since he had watched him parade through the streets of New York in May 1919. Struck by the intense reaction of his own employees to the mountaineer hero, Lasky immediately dispatched a representative to the Waldorf-Astoria to make him an offer. York refused, but the persistent Lasky contacted him again some ten years later only to find York still opposed to the idea.[11]

Realizing the potential impact of the story and desperately in need of a vehicle that would enable him to reenter the motion picture business, Lasky turned once more to the York project in 1939. He sent a letter to York, tactfully suggesting the possiblity of a film, but York did not reply. Undeterred, Lasky then dispatched a telegram asking for a conference to discuss "a historical document of vital importance to the country in these troubled times." Aware that his man would not accept a proposal that smacked of commercialism, Lasky's strategy was similar to the one used earlier by Skeyhill, namely, to create a conflict of values in York's mind by challenging his aversion to self-aggrandizement with his sense of duty to religious and patriotic causes. Predictably, the appeal to patriotism struck a responsive chord in York, who advocated preparedness in the face of the growing foreign threat. Also, Lasky's proposal came at a time when York was planning an interdenominational Bible school designed to "prepare its pupils to live and practice a full Christian life." Envisioning a school where the "pioneer faith will be kept burning," York intended to construct the facility in Fentress County as a complement to his high school, the York Agricultural Institute. Needing money for the project, York was now willing to reconsider a position he had staunchly held for twenty years, and he agreed to see Lasky.[12]

The two men met in a Crossville, Tennessee, hotel on March 9, 1940. To York's surprise, the press was waiting for him when he strode into the lobby. Wincing as photographers snapped his picture, he said apologetically, "I don't have my Sunday clothes on," and explained that he and Lasky were simply "renewing an old acquaintance," although reporters noted that neither man recognized the other until they were introduced. They conferred briefly in private before York took his visitor on a tour of Fentress County with special stops at the York Agricultural Institute and the site of the future

Bible school. Getting the producer interested in his schools was important, York told interviewers, because "$50,000 to men like Lasky is the same as 50¢ to me." York was less explicit about the details of the negotiations. "All I know about this movie job," he said, "is that Mr. Lasky visited me . . . , went with me to the old home place where I am planning to start work on my new Bible school soon, and left after making me an attractive offer which will not require a great deal of my time away from home."[13]

By Thursday, March 14, Lasky was back in Tennessee to meet York and Jamestown attorney John Hale at the Hermitage Hotel in Nashville. "What we want," Hale told Lasky, "is a plain old Tennessee contract that simply says what you shall do and what the sergeant shall do." York was equally direct. "You know there isn't a great deal of difference between trading for a mule or a movie contract," he said. "What really counts is the trader." York's major concern was achieving a financial arrangement that would provide enough money to build the Bible school. Lasky initially offered twenty-five thousand and then fifty thousand dollars, but York insisted on a percentage of the gross receipts as well. During a brief interlude in the discussions, Lasky and York strolled up to the capitol to visit York's friend and informal advisor, Governor Prentice Cooper. "He urged Sergeant York to go ahead with it and gave the picture his blessing," Lasky reported, but the two sides still could not reconcile their differences. Periodically the sergeant would leave Lasky's room and mysteriously vanish down the hall while the argument sputtered on. Curious, Lasky at last followed him and discovered York kneeling in prayer. Impressed by York's piety yet frustrated by his stubbornness, on Saturday Lasky returned to Hollywood to weigh the matter. Finally, a week later, Lasky made another trip east to accept York's terms and join him in a contract-signing ceremony in Governor Cooper's office. York would receive fifty thousand dollars plus 2 percent of the gross, a figure that was expected to be roughly one hundred thousand dollars.[14]

Both York and Lasky made it clear that they intended the

film to be a special one despite the different perspectives they had on the project. "I wish to emphasize that this is in no sense a war picture," Lasky said, although he definitely saw the propaganda value of the York story. Describing the film as an example of "the historical medium of the future," Lasky termed it "a story Americans need to be told today." York's biography "will be a document for fundamental Americanism" and "the story of a great personality from which Americans will draw inspiration." York, however, expected a film that would use his experiences to tell the story of the mountain people. "Actually it's going to be more a story of our people up there in the mountains than it is of me," he said. "It's going to show how education has been taken into the mountains and how we're training our young people now to be good citizens." Asserting that he did not like "war pictures," York said, "My part in the war should be presented only as an incident in my life. The way I've lived since then, the contributions I've made to my community, are the things I'm really proud of."[15]

Implicit in the remarks of each man is the notion that Appalachia is somehow a special repository of "fundamental Americanism," a notion that had also influenced Cowan and Skeyhill. As an editorial in the Nashville *Tennessean* put it, " . . . the time is ripe for a reminder that the pioneer spirit still survives." Isolated and rather backward, the mountains had supposedly escaped the corrupting influences of urban-industrial society and preserved traditional American values in their purest form. " . . . [I]n this day of uncertainty in our great democracy," the *Tennessean* observed, "there is need of reassurance that the Tall Men still are a vital part of American life." To Jesse Lasky and millions of other Americans, Sergeant York and his neighbors were the contemporary heirs of the spirit that had made America great.[16]

The filming of *Sergeant York* presented Lasky with a number of perplexing problems, the most immediate of which was finding a studio that would take it on. As proof of good faith, Lasky gave York a postdated check for twenty-five thousand dollars, disregarding the fact that his financial situation was so precarious he had to borrow on his life insurance to cover it. With the rest of the fifty thousand dollars due sixty days after the signing, Lasky crisscrossed Hollywood in search of a backer, but his efforts were unsuccessful because war movies were usually weak at the box office. Finally a friend suggested that Harry Warner of Warner Brothers was particularly susceptible to projects with a patriotic theme. Warner was intrigued by the idea and promised to give it serious consideration if Lasky could line up some talent. Encouraged, Lasky invited Howard Hawks to direct. Uninterested in screen biographies, Hawks was reluctant to accept until Lasky convinced him that *Sergeant York* would not follow the standard success story format for such films. Disavowing the usual cliché-ridden approach, Lasky told Hawks he was planning a character study of York rather than a simple description of his life. As Hawks explained the technique, "I don't attempt to preach or prove anything. I just figure out what I think was in the man and tell it." Persuaded by Lasky, Hawks cancelled his commitment to direct *The Outlaw* for Howard Hughes and signed for *Sergeant York*. With Hawks aboard, Warner Brothers accepted the film and added Hal Wallis as coproducer with Lasky.[17]

Casting the part of Alvin York was particularly difficult. Most press speculation centered on four actors, Gary Cooper, Henry Fonda, Raymond Massey, and Spencer Tracy, although columnist Louella Parsons cautioned her readers not to "faint from surprise if it turns out to be Jimmy Cagney." Pondering the idea of Cagney as the lanky mountaineer moved the *Tennessean* to editorialize, "We'll faint if it's Jimmy." From the first, though, Lasky wanted Gary Cooper for the lead and set out to trap the star. Leaving Nashville after signing the contract with York, Lasky hastily composed a telegram to Cooper: "I have just agreed to let the motion picture producer Jesse L. Lasky film the story of my life, subject to my approval of the star. I have great admiration for you as an actor and as a man, and I would be honored, sir, to see you on the screen as myself." He signed York's name to it and sent it off, thereby planting the idea that Cooper was York's personal choice for the role.[18]

The offer brought Cooper what he later called "my first

big struggle with my responsibility to the movie going public." Aware of the patriotic merit of the movie, he nevertheless believed that York was too complex a man for him to portray adequately. "Here was a pious, sincere man, a conscientious objector to war, who, when called, became a heroic fighter for his country," Cooper wrote later. "He was too big for me, he covered too much territory." Still he realized that with the "clouds of World War II piling up fast, . . . what had happened to Sergeant York was likely to happen all over again." Cooper's worries were compounded by the fact that York, unlike most subjects of screen biographies, was still alive and very much concerned about the accuracy of the finished film. York's attitude precluded what Cooper called the "romantic leeway" that was customary in "screen biographies dealing with remote historical characters." Cooper concluded that he "couldn't handle it."[19]

Undeterred by his refusal, Hawks and Lasky pressured Cooper to change his mind. Hawks reminded him that Lasky had helped launch the actor's career while an executive at Paramount, and Lasky arranged a series of "chance" encounters with Cooper that gave him an opportunity to discuss the matter at length. Finally Cooper agreed, providing that MGM, the studio holding his contract, would release him temporarily to Warner Brothers, a deal finalized in early September when Sam Goldwyn agreed to loan Cooper to Warner Brothers in exchange for permission to use Warner star Bette Davis in *The Little Foxes*. Aside from the title role, York was concerned only with the casting of the part of Gracie Williams, his sweetheart and future wife. He and Mrs. York insisted that the actress selected to portray her must not smoke or drink, a potentially tough order to fill in jaded Hollywood. Lasky wanted Jane Russell, an actress still awaiting her first screen role, but Warner Brothers chose one of its own contract players, a sixteen-year-old fledgling named Joan Leslie. She was joined by Walter Brennan as York's minister, Pastor Rosier Pile, and Margaret Wycherly as his mother, the other leading characters.[20]

Because *Sergeant York* was about a living man, its shooting presented a unique problem, namely, the need to obtain release from all the people it would portray who were still alive. William Guthrie, location manager for Warner, traveled ten thousand miles tracking down the members of York's squad. He managed to find ten of them holding such diverse jobs as insurance salesman, honky-tonk waiter, and orange grower. One man was eking out a five-dollar-a-week existence by salvaging metal from the Philadelphia city dump, while another was wanted by the police and had to be contacted through a newspaper advertisement. Guthrie paid each one $250 for permission to portray him on the screen. York's friends and relatives in Fentress County negotiated shrewdly with Guthrie, some winning fees as high as $1,500 for their cooperation. York's father-in-law, however, refused to sign, and his character was deleted from the script.[21]

Lasky and Warner Brothers took pains to satisfy York's demands for accuracy. On April 21, barely a month after the contract was signed, Lasky, a cameraman, and two writers arrived in Pall Mall to collect background information about their subject. They stayed a week, visiting a shooting match and interviewing two hundred people. A few months later, Lasky brought York to Hollywood where he previewed the script and then called on Gary Cooper to give the actor a chance to become better acquainted with the character he would have to recreate on the screen. As York and Cooper sat silently in the latter's living room, the gregarious Lasky desperately tried to spark a conversation. "If we'd had Calvin Coolidge there," Lasky remembered, "it would have been a three-ring wake." Finally Lasky mentioned Cooper's gun collection and then sat back as the two hunters eagerly discussed the relative merits of their favorite weapons. "Sergeant York and I had quite a few things in common . . . ," Cooper later wrote. "We both were raised in the mountains —Tennessee for him, Montana for me— and learned to ride and shoot as a natural part of growing up." Asked his opinion of the Westerner, York bluntly replied, "He's a good shot."[22]

Their field work done, Lasky's production team set out to recreate a slice of Fentress County life in a Hollywood sound studio. The 123 sets were a record number, as was the number of living people being portrayed, and the script included more speaking parts than any picture up to that time except *Anthony Adverse*. The crew took over the largest stage in town, building a forty-foot mountain made of timber, cloth, plaster, rock, soil, and 121 live trees. Mounted on a turntable, it had sixteen faces and was equipped with spare peaks and precipices to replace any that might break. An unexpected problem developed with the score: it called for a baying dog, but Warner Brothers discovered to its dismay that none of its trained animals bayed in the required key of A. Fortunately, a hastily arranged screen test at the local pound resulted in the "discovery" of a suitably talented canine. The battle scenes were filmed in a field forty miles away where, Cooper said, "We blew up enough land . . . to make a good-sized farm in Iowa." The hectic ninety-day shooting schedule was made even more frenzied by the lack of a completed script. The original script by Abem Finkel and Harry Chandlee was later revised by John Huston and Howard Koch, although, in the end, Hawks said he and Huston "threw away the written script and did what Jesse Lasky told us about the real Sergeant York." The two "just kept ahead of shooting," according to Hawks, leaving the director uncertain of how the finished product would look, especially since, as he put it, the film "follows no patterns."[23]

The publicity connected with the filming catapulted York into the limelight and gave him an opportunity to express his views concerning national defense and foreign policy. Like many people, he believed that if America simply supplied arms to Great Britain, John Bull could dispose of Hitler and Germany without any direct intervention by the United States. In January 1941, he lauded Franklin Roosevelt's "arsenal of democracy" address as "one of the greatest speeches I've ever heard" because the president "was giving the American people the truth straight from the shoulder." Speaking before the alumni banquet of the York Agricultural Institute a few months later, York derided the "calamity howlers who are shouting from the housetops that Hitler cannot be beaten," and declared, " . . . Hitler can, will, and must be beaten. We must give all-out aid to Great Britain, even if we have to convoy our cargoes right to the English shore." On May 30, York gave the Memorial Day address at the Tomb of the Unknown Soldier, the anonymous symbol of the nation's war dead. In his widely reported remarks he launched a fierce attack on the isolationists, particularly Senator Burton K. Wheeler whom York disdainfully nicknamed "Neville" after the discredited British prime minister Neville Chamberlain. "The senator ought to know by now," York declared, "that you can't protect yourself against bullets with an umbrella." In earnest tones he tried to explain how he felt about his own wartime service:

> There are those in this country today who ask me and other veterans of World War Number One, 'What did it get you?' . . . The thing they forget is that liberty and freedom and democracy are so very precious that you do not fight to win them once and stop. You do not do that. Liberty and freedom and democracy are prizes awarded only to those peoples who fight to win them and then keep fighting eternally to hold them!

A few months later York noticed with pride that Roosevelt had quoted him extensively in the president's Armistice Day remarks to the nation.[24]

The glittering New York premiere of *Sergeant York* provided the Tennessean with yet another chance to urge preparedness. He arrived in New York on July 1 for a five-day visit studded with frequent press conferences. Once again he had harsh words for the isolationists, saying, "I think any man who talks against the interest of his own country ought to be arrested and put in jail, not excepting senators and ex-colonels," explicit references to Wheeler and America First spokesman Colonel Charles A. Lindbergh. Asked about Herbert Hoover's criticism of American foreign policy, York snorted, "Hoover doesn't know the temper of the people. That's why he's an ex-President." York insisted there would

be no reason to send a second American Expeditionary Force
to Europe if the United States kept Britain supplied. "It is my
honest conviction," he said, "that England does not need our
manpower over there. What she needs is our manpower over
here, producing planes and guns and tanks and boats." To
assure the safe arrival of the supplies, the United States should
"bust up all of old man Hitler's ships and submarines." In
York's view, "We should clear the Atlantic right away. It's
nonsense to make our material here and have it go to the
bottom."[25]

Sergeant York opened July 2 at the Astor Theater where
several hundred people cheered York's arrival and an enthusiastic audience gave him a fifteen-minute ovation after
the show. Asked to say a few words, the sergeant expressed
his hope that the film would contribute to "national unity
in this hour of danger" when "millions of Americans, like
myself, must be facing the same questions, the same uncertainties, which we faced and I believe resolved for the right
some twenty-four years ago."[26]

A month later, on July 30, York, Lasky, Gary Cooper, and
Tennessee Senator Kenneth McKellar visited President
Roosevelt at the White House during the film's Washington
premiere. Eager to identify his controversial foreign policy
with a popular hero, FDR said he had had a special preview
ten days earlier and was "really thrilled" by it. "The picture
comes at a good time," the president continued, "although
I didn't like that part of it showing so much killing. I guess
you felt that way too." "I certainly did," York replied. The
president puckishly expressed his regret that "old Cordell,"
meaning Cordell Hull, now secretary of state, could not have
played his own part as the then congressman from York's
district. The ten-minute session ended with York, to
Roosevelt's obvious delight, assuring the chief executive that
the people of Tennessee were solidly behind his policies.[27]

Contemporary reactions to the film were strongly influenced by the bitter debate over foreign policy. Preparedness
advocates hailed it as a vital and important film. "Like the
clear notes of reveille at summer sunrise," said *Variety*,
"*Sergeant York* is a clarion film that reaches the public at a

moment when its stirring and patriotic message is probably most needed." The show business weekly predicted that *York* "will hit box offices like a hand grenade." Labeling Jesse Lasky "as sincere a movie maker as Hollywood ever knew," *Life* explicitly connected York's experience with the events of 1941, saying, "York, as played by Cooper, had to solve certain personal problems about the last World War, just as other Americans must solve personal problems about the war of today." *Time* called it "Hollywood's first solid contribution to the national defense," and Senator McKellar told his colleagues, "I believe it will be of enormous benefit to citizens of the United States of America to see the picture."[28]

By contrast, isolationists were sharply critical of the film. Writing in the *New Republic*, reviewer Otis Ferguson dismissed it as a "stunt picture" about a feat that "did nothing toward winning" a war that "made far greater demands in the way of day-in-day-out heroism." Speaking to an America First rally in St. Louis, North Dakota Senator Gerald P. Nye warned, 'The movies have ceased to be an instrument of entertainment," and instead "have been operating as war propaganda machines almost as if they were directed from a single central bureau." Nye noted that Roosevelt himself "after he had forced Congress to pass the lend-lease bill . . . complimented the industry on their 'help' in explaining the bill." Referring to York's visit to the White House, he remarked that if FDR did not like the killing shown on the screen he was nevertheless willing to see the film arouse people to kill.[29]

In spite of the political debate *Sergeant York* provoked, many reviewers found themes in the movie besides preparedness. *New York Times* critic Bosley Crowther called it an "honest saga of a plain American who believed in fundamentals and acted with a clear simplicity." The film was a "simple and dignified screen biography" that "has all the flavor of true Americana." Howard Barnes of the New York *Herald Tribune* described it as a "stirring saga of Southern hillfolk" complete with "shots of ploughing and log-splitting which are almost documentary." Even without the war scenes, Barnes concluded, *Sergeant York* was a "valiant testament to the American way of life." Southerners particularly liked the film because it cast the South in such a favorable light. The Nashville *Tennessean* praised *York* as an "antidote for the poison of *Tobacco Road*" and noted "the fresh appreciation of the East for the tale of the Tennessee doughboy."[30]

York, his family, and his friends were quite pleased with the picture. The sergeant pronounced it a "fine job," chuckling, "Gary Cooper had me like I was years ago when I weighed only 170 pounds." The two decades since then had added over a hundred pounds to York's now portly frame. Vehemently denying that it was a propaganda film, York said the only people who felt that way were "definitely Nazi inclined themselves." Pastor Rosier Pile was also pleased with the work of Walter Brennan in the role of York's minister. "That fellow who played me put over what I was trying to get over to Alvin," he said. Least impressed was probably Gracie Williams York. When Joan Leslie telephoned from Hollywood to ask if she was excited by the Nashville premiere, Mrs. York replied, "Oh, no, I'm used to this." She admitted that "most of the facts were pretty accurate" and that seeing it "sure carries me back," but Mrs. York was a shy, private woman who took little delight in her husband's celebrity status. In fact, she had refused to accompany him to California for fear they might both be killed in an accident and their children orphaned.[31]

York's single objection to the film centered on the portrayal of his religious conversion. During one of their conversations, Howard Hawks asked him how he had gotten religion, and York said he had found it "in the middle of the road," a cryptic comment the director took literally. The movie shows Gary Cooper being struck by a bolt of lightning while riding to kill a man who has cheated him. The stunned Cooper then wanders into a church and is "saved." York, however, understood things differently:

> That weren't the right down facts of it. You see I had met Miss Gracie. Miss Gracie said that she wouldn't let me come a-courting until I'd quit my mean drinking, fighting, and card-flipping. So you see I was struck down

by the power of love and the Great God Almighty, all together. A bolt of lightning was the nearest to such a thing that Hollywood could think up.

Despite the misunderstanding, neither York nor his wife was perturbed by the scene because, as Miss Gracie put it, "that was just demonstrating the power of the Lord."[32]

Sergeant York brought important benefits for many of the people connected with it. His career rejuvenated, Jesse Lasky made roughly five hundred thousand dollars from his brainchild. The film was Howard Hawks's greatest commercial success and earned him the only Academy Award nomination he ever received. Even more fortunate was Gary Cooper, who drew high critical acclaim and won the first of two Oscars for best performance by an actor. "I put all I had into the role," Cooper admitted, but he insisted, "I didn't win that award. Sergeant York did, because to the best of my ability I was him." Alvin York's rewards were less spectacular yet equally gratifying. The one hundred fifty thousand dollars the film earned for him stabilized his financial situation and enabled him to begin the preliminary work on his Bible school.[33]

In the years since its release, *Sergeant York* has remained popular with audiences, but critics have expressed substantial doubt about its artistic quality. One Hawks scholar groups it and *Land of the Pharoahs* together as the director's only two failures, while others have stressed the essentially tragic conclusion of the film. As critic Andrew Sarris noted, "It is a sad ending for a man of conviction to be rewarded for his murders." Howard Hawks himself admitted, "We tried to show a bewildered man." The view was strengthened during the 1960s by the protest against American involvement in Vietnam. Standing the film on its head, the protestors argued that York's true heroism was expressed by his initial pacifism, not by his duel with the machine guns in the Argonne. One advertisement for a campus showing of *Sergeant York* presented it as "the paradox of a conscientious objector becoming a mass killer."[34]

Whatever its cinematic flaws might be, *Sergeant York* was

a huge success on its own terms. The film made a great deal of money and proved to be a very effective propaganda device. "[I]t turned out to be a hell of a picture . . . ," Howard Hawks said, "and we had no idea it was going to be anything like that." Unfortunately, however, like the books it drew on, the film simply ignored uncomfortable truths about the real Alvin York. Its basic message is that York made a morally correct decision to participate in a just war, and his nation rewarded him for his efforts. The point becomes explicit in the last scene of the film, which shows York and Gracie Williams standing in front of a new house on a fully stocked farm given to them by the people of Tennessee. By implication, of course, such rewards are the lot of dutiful soldiers, but, as we have already discussed, York actually returned to four hundred undeveloped and mortgaged acres, a farm York nearly had to pay for himself.[35]

Besides ignoring the facts, the film buttressed its theme by using some obvious devices to manipulate audiences. York's innocence was underscored by presenting an idealized, stereotyped view of his Appalachian origins. A German prisoner who treacherously kills York's buddy "Pusher" serves to remind us of German bestiality. The incident, of course, is fictitious. The score repeatedly intermingles religious and patriotic melodies to suggest divine blessing on American arms. The result is a powerful and sophisticated call to the colors that had a lasting impact on the audiences who saw it. The film proved to be such a powerful legend maker that even members of York's own family were influenced by it. One of its scenes shows York gobbling like a turkey at the German gunners to get them to raise their heads so he can shoot them. The gobbling is probably a cinematic device—York never made any reference to such tactics in his various accounts of the battle—but at least one of York's sons accepts the scene as true.[36]

By 1941, then, the legend makers had completed their work. York was permanently established as a national hero whose name was synonymous with patriotism, piety, and marksmanship. In the process, however, the human being himself—his character, his beliefs, even the circumstances of his life—were tailored to the purposes of the legend. Yet, in a very real sense, the truth about Alvin York is not particularly important. The legend makers did not distort their subject out of malice but rather as part of an effort to reassure their fellow citizens that certain traditional values still thrived in the republic. They created a hero in response to a felt need in society, and Alvin York answered that need. His significance lies not in what he was but in what others wanted to make of him. His willingness to submit to such a process was a greater service than the one he rendered in the Argonne Forest.

7. Last Years

The making of *Sergeant York* reconfirmed Alvin York's status as an American hero and restored him to public prominence, but in many ways his life remained unchanged. Just as he had done for twenty years, York continued to turn his fame toward the service of the causes he most cherished, patriotism, religious education, and regional development. Although the neglect of his personal needs eventually brought him again to the brink of financial ruin, his popularity never faltered. Until his death in 1964, Americans continued to see him as a man who represented the finest elements of the national character. Interestingly enough, however, York's antiwar feelings vanished without a trace in the years after 1941, and the former pacifist became an outspoken advocate of violent solutions to America's international problems. Perhaps such a change was only to be expected in a man who had been so praised for his military prowess, but the bellicose old soldier is a sad contrast with the innocent young draftee who could not reconcile killing and Christianity.

Only five months after the premiere of *Sergeant York*, the Japanese attack on Pearl Harbor brought the United States into the Second World War. Eager for a combat role, York registered for the draft on April 27, 1942, in the same general store where he had registered twenty-five years earlier. Pastor Pile still served as clerk. "If they want me for active duty, I'm ready to go," he said. "I'm in a mighty different mood now from that other time." York was particularly concerned about the number of Fentress County men being rejected for service because they were illiterate. Describing his fellow mountaineers as "crack shots" and the "best soldiers in the world," he assured the War Department that "everyone of them will be able to endorse his first army paycheck." As proof of his conviction, York offered to lead a battalion of Kentucky and Tennessee illiterates into battle. Although the War Department gave him a special commission as a major charged with infantry problems, York's chance for active service faded when he failed the physical examination. Overweight and suffering from arthritic twinges, York admitted that he could not hike, but countered that he could still drive a tank and boasted that if he had had the army's new M-1 rifle none of the Germans would have escaped him in the Argonne. Despite his protests, the army denied him regular military service.[1]

Disappointed, York threw himself into volunteer work to support the war effort. Perhaps his most important post was chairman of the Fentress County Selective Service Board, the body that drafted young men for the armed services. Among those it had called to service by 1945 were two of York's sons. Between meetings, York accepted countless invitations to tour training camps or participate in bond drives, usually traveling at his own expense. Concerned that America's soldiers be drilled in "liquor-free, wholesome, and clean surroundings," he told the new recruits to keep their Bibles with them and "get as many [of the enemy] as they could" when they were sent into combat. York also did fundraising for such war-related charities as the Red Cross, urging potential contributors to be generous because "next to his own mother and sweetheart, the Red Cross is the soldier's best friend." In addition, York loaned his name to a syndicated column, "Sergeant York Says," which appeared regularly in newspapers across the country. Although he was a personable and loquacious man, York was not interested in writing, so composition of the column invariably fell to others who sought to foster patriotism in the folksy style the public had come to associate with Alvin York.[2]

York's concern for the individual GI often led him to in-

tervene with the civilian and military bureaucracy on behalf
of soldiers with problems. This was especially true if the man
hailed from the Tennessee mountains. Learning that a local
enlisted man was about to be executed for a murder he had
committed in the South Pacific, York wrote to President
Harry S. Truman to plead for a commuted sentence, explaining, "I am well acquainted with the soldier's family and
believe that his three years of volunteer service in the army
merits your highest consideration." In another case, York took
up the cause of a young soldier sentenced to fifteen years in
prison for attempting to rape what York called "an English
bar-room girl." "The boy tore the girl's clothes . . . ," York admitted, "but from my observation and experience in England
in the First World War, as I am sure was yours also, we know
how rough and tough some of those English girls could be."
Despite York's pleas, Truman refused to interfere with either
sentence.[3]

York's importance as a symbolic figure, an image enhanced
by the release of the film, made him very popular, particularly in the early months of the war. The string of defeats from
Hawaii to the Philippines bred few heroes, so York, as the
most famous hero of the last war, became a special target of
publicity. For example, his efforts to obtain a combat assignment and subsequent commissioning as a major received considerable attention in the press. Also, he accepted the national
chairmanship of a citizens' committee working to persuade
every American to display the flag in his home. York promptly
enlisted General Douglas MacArthur in the effort, asking him
to accept the post of "honorary international commander in
chief." MacArthur accepted with a "sense of distinction," wiring York, "Throughout the history of mankind symbols have
exerted an impelling influence upon the lives of men. The
cross and the flag are embodiments of our ideals and teach
us not only how to live but how to die." Through it all, York
salted his public comments with fighting rhetoric and general
support for the Roosevelt Administration. Tennessee Valley
Authority board member David Lilienthal listened to a radio
broadcast of York preaching to a small mountain congrega-

tion and noted in his diary the thrill he felt hearing this "man of the mountains" declare that some evil "was goin' to be stomped out." In a rousing speech to a hundred dollar-a-plate Democratic fund raiser attended by Vice President Henry A. Wallace, Speaker Sam Rayburn, and Mrs. Eleanor Roosevelt, he called for prompt offensive action against the enemy and urged, "Let us go get Douglas MacArthur and bring him out of the Philippines — we need his advice and counsel." He went on to warn against a fifth column in the United States, saying all aliens should be rounded up and put in camps guarded by World War I veterans. Like many Americans, he was particularly suspicious of the Japanese who, "whether native or foreign born, all look alike and we can't take any chances."[4]

York graphically demonstrated his value as a symbol while visiting Camp Claiborne, Louisiana, where the Eighty-second Division was being reactivated. Its commander, Major General Omar N. Bradley, was anxious to build the spirit and morale of his fledgling unit, so he and his second-in-command, Matthew Ridgway, invited York to tour the post and address the troops. A division review staged in his honor drew considerable media attention, and York's speech to the new soldiers was carried live on a nationwide hookup. Besides building morale, York's trip also had a tangible impact on the training the Eighty-second received in the future. Bradley, who had never been in combat, quizzed York closely about his experiences in France and learned that most of the sergeant's effective shooting had been done at short range, twenty-five to fifty yards. "As a result of these talks," Bradley later wrote, "I had the staff set up a short-range firing course in the woods with partially concealed cans for targets. The men had to traverse this wooded course, spot the cans and shoot quickly. It was a radical departure from the standard static long-distance firing range." Ridgway believed that York "had a great deal to do with the early inculcation of that supreme confidence, that magnificant *esprit*, which later was to be the hallmark of the airborne." York, according to Ridgway, "created in the minds of farm boys and clerks, youngsters of every station and class, the conviction that an aggressive soldier, well trained and well armed, can fight his way out of any situation." Bradley agreed with Ridgway's assessment that York's visit "was a tremendous morale builder for the troops," but, Bradley concluded, "he surely deflated me." Taking leave of his host, York had told the future five-star general he would not get very far in this world because Bradley was "too nice."[5]

The wartime crisis prompted York to consider a role in elective politics. In 1936, he had been nominated for vice president on the Prohibition Party ticket, but he declined, saying, "If I ever run for anything it will be on the Democratic ticket. I'm a Democrat first, last, and all the time." Four years later he had considered running for Congress but other responsibilities had intruded on his plans. Through the early months of the year, his job as a project director for the Civilian Conservation Corps made him subject to the Hatch Act, which barred political activity by federal employees. Just as the job expired, he began work on the movie and simply had no time to mount a campaign for the August primary. With his popularity soaring as *Sergeant York* played to enthusiastic audiences around the country, York once again considered a run for the House of Representatives against incumbent Albert Gore. "I figure Albert Gore is young and could fill a place in the fighting forces," York said. "So it looks like it might be a good thing if I could take his place in Congress." Never explaining why, however, York did not file for the office. Throughout his adult life, York periodically contemplated elective politics only to decide finally that he was not interested. Although he never actually explained his attitude, several factors probably influenced his thinking. First of all, serving in any state or national office would involve an extended absence from home, something York always tried to avoid. Beyond this, until World War II, the only public issue that genuinely concerned him was education, and holding an elective office could only interfere with the work he was already doing as a private citizen. In addition, York may have concluded that seeking office would simply be another form of commercializing his fame. The Nashville *Banner* expressed the feelings of many in an editorial asking York not to run in 1942: "Ex-soldiers in politics are a dime a dozen, whereas there is only one Hero Alvin York. It does not follow—moreover, that a good soldier makes a statesman." Whatever his thinking, York decided to pass up his political opportunities.[6]

Not surprisingly, York's position as the nation's most acclaimed citizen-soldier was challenged somewhat during the war years by the growing popularity of more recent heroes, especially Lieutenant Audie Murphy. One of eleven children born to the family of a Texas sharecropper, Murphy saw World War II as his chance to escape rural poverty. Not yet eighteen in early 1942, he lied about his age and weight in order to enlist. The marines and the paratroopers rejected him,, but the determined Murphy finally won an assignment as an army infantryman. He saw extensive combat in North Africa, Italy, and France and was credited with killing 240 German soldiers. During the January 1945 advance through the Colmar Pocket in eastern France, Murphy and his company found themselves under assault by six tanks and waves of German infantry. Murphy ordered his men to retreat while he stayed behind to direct an artillery bombardment. Leaping atop a burning American tank, he turned its .50 caliber machine gun on the Germans and held his position for an hour amid enemy fire from three sides. He then led his men in a counterattack that secured the position. His feat earned him the Medal of Honor and twenty-seven other medals as well, making him the most decorated American combat soldier of the war.[7]

Murphy paid a high price for his valor. Of the 235 men originally assigned to his company, only Murphy and one other man were still in the outfit when the war ended. His division suffered total casualties amounting to three times its authorized strength. After the war, Murphy was tortured by nightmares for years and could sleep only with a loaded German Walther automatic pistol tucked under his pillow. Medals meant little to him after the horrors he had witnessed, and he gave most of them away to children. Thanks to the prominence his combat career brought him, however, he became a screen actor in the late 1940s, playing mostly soldiers and cowboys in films of little merit. His career faded as the film industry changed in the mid-1960s, and Murphy declared bankruptcy in 1968. He was working in the investment business when he was killed in a 1971 plane crash.[8]

York and Murphy are similar in several superficial ways. Both were southerners who were born into large families and raised in poverty. As youngsters both of them hunted out of necessity rather than for sport and became very skillful with weapons. Although Murphy's battlefield exploits eventually won him a commission, like Alvin York he spent most of his military career as an enlisted man. Both men won the Medal of Honor for feats they performed late in the wars in which they participated. York and Murphy published books about their exploits which were later made into successful movies. Also, both of them experienced serious financial difficulties later in life.

But whatever their similarities, York and Murphy were profoundly different people. One crucial difference centers on their evolving attitudes toward war. Although Murphy enlisted eagerly for combat duty, fighting left him emotionally spent. Killing with the efficiency of a machine simply because he knew no other way to survive, he had no thoughts about doing his patriotic duty or performing the will of God. Murphy simply wanted to come out of the war alive and in one piece.

This feeling comes through sharply in Murphy's 1949 memoir, *To Hell and Back*. Needing money after his discharge, he wrote the book himself in longhand, although a professional writer has obviously reworked the basic material. Gritty, realistic, and vivid, *To Hell and Back* received good notices for its harsh portrayal of army life. *Saturday Review* called it "a terrible, powerful book," and the New York *Herald Tribune* praised its "unadorned and authentic style." According to the *New York Times*, Murphy had written "one excellent war story." The book describes World War II through the eyes of a combat infantryman. High-ranking officers rarely intrude, and Murphy devotes little time to grand strategy. He mentions none of his medals and passes quickly over his promotion to second lieutenant. None of this is particularly meaningful to him. Instead, he describes in terse, laconic prose what modern warfare is like for the front-line soldier.[9]

Murphy's view of World War II stands in striking contrast to York's view of World War I. Compared with Murphy's tour, York's combat service was fairly brief. He arrived in France less than six months before the Armistice, whereas Murphy spent over two years in combat zones and saw a good deal more action than York had. Consequently, York's experience was somewhat less traumatic. After initially dreading military service, he ultimately became a strong champion of the armed services. Murphy's combat experiences, by contrast, soured his youthful enthusiasm and left him bitterly aware of the human cost that modern warfare exacted. The memoirs both men prepared clearly reflect their different perceptions. The book York wrote with Thomas Skeyhill is essentially a religiopatriotic tract. It discusses death but spares readers the grim details that pervade Murphy's account. York's military service is essentially an exercise in idealism, while Murphy mentions God only when he is swearing. Moreover, Murphy seems to define himself almost totally by his combat experience. York's book provides considerable detail about his home and family, but Murphy says virtually nothing about his life away from the front.

Clearly the America that hailed Audie Murphy in 1945 was quite different from the nation that cheered Alvin York in 1919. Most obviously, the Second World War gave rise to a realism that qualified the old platitudes about God and country. Most Americans certainly felt their cause was just, but neither Audie Murphy nor many of his buddies saw the hand of God guiding events. Moreover, like many postwar Americans, Murphy was a rootless character with weak family and community ties. He lacked York's strong identification with his native region and his commitment to community service. Eventually Murphy selected the option York had renounced in 1919 and began to commercialize himself, especially

through the entertainment world. He did not represent the
stability and certainty that many of his countrymen wanted
to see reaffirmed. As a result, Murphy is less valuable as a
national symbol than York is. Although Murphy ends *To Hell
and Back* with a few sentences extolling patriotism and the
middle-class life-style, the main thrust of the book is better
expressed by Murphy's GI catechism: "I believe in the force
of a hand grenade, the power of artillery, the accuracy of a
Garand. I believe in hitting before you get hit, and that dead
men do not look noble." Such cynicism is not the stuff of
popular heroes.[10]

Beyond his cynicism, Murphy also differed from York in
his introspection. Much more than York, Murphy expressed
concern about what the war had done to him as a human being. Sitting in a Cannes hotel on VE Day, Murphy caressed
his service revolver, finding it "more beautiful than a flower;
more faithful than most friends." As the horrors he had seen
flickered through his mind, Murphy compared the war to a
fire that had "roared through this human house, leaving only
the charred hulk of something that once was green." At the
end of his book, he frankly confesses he does not know how
to live in a world at peace. York, by contrast, admits to none
of these feelings. Claiming to serve as the instrument of God
in a holy cause, he cannot admit that military service
coarsened him or challenged his basic beliefs. Indeed, one of
the major themes of the York legend is that the Tennessean
is unchanged either by public acclaim or the horrors of war.
He smoothly reenters the society that spawned him by marrying his sweetheart and settling down to farm and raise a family. York certainly must have shared some of Murphy's feelings, but they never became part of his public image. When
a Nashville newspaperman wrote an article about York in
which the sergeant discussed the war's impact on his health
and expressed his doubts about American involvement, the
writer's paper declined to run it. Such self-scrutiny was apparently considered inappropriate in a national hero of York's
stature.[11]

In the years after World War II, York continued to speak

out concerning public issues, especially those related to defense, but the pacifist of 1917 had changed greatly in the course of thirty years. Like many Americans, he saw the Soviet Union as a major threat to the United States and fretted that America was not effectively confronting the Communist challenge. "We are going to have to fight for our lives," he warned a 1947 American Legion meeting, "and we better be ready." He charged that the "thumb-twiddlers" in Washington would be better hog callers than policymakers and told a *New York Times* reporter, "We've got to take a firm stand with Russia. We found out what appeasement got us from Japan." York's prescription for international accord reflected the combination of piety and militancy so characteristic of his public image. He still believed that religion was "the only real solution for all problems—personal, social, and international," but he had no reservations about using the atomic bomb to provide a more immediate remedy. "I wouldn't give one American boy for everything I've seen in Europe," he declared, asserting that the best way to deter the Soviets was to "let the atomic bomb do the job." We should "wipe them from the face of the earth in one terrific blow," he insisted, "and let's do it in time to save ourselves." The ex-infantryman offered to fire the first shot, saying, "If they can't find anyone else to push the button, I will."[12]

The outbreak of the Korean War in June 1950 only enhanced York's belligerency. Convinced that the Soviets were to blame for the North Korean attack, York urged America to "start at Joseph Stalin's and go on down 'til we burn 'em all up—atomic bomb and all." A year later, with the war a bloody stalemate along the 38th Parallel, York wrote President Truman to ask why the United Nations forces did not employ the weapon to break the deadlock. Only partially mollified by Truman's explanation that an atomic blast would kill friendly as well as enemy forces, York argued, "We are going to have to go to Moscow to win the war. Let's take an A-bomb and go up to the head of the spring and muddy the waters."[13]

The frustrations of the early 1950s turned York's thinking

again to politics. Since flirting with the idea of running for
Congress a decade earlier, he had shied away from seeking
public office because, "I think it is better to leave that to the
young folks," but in 1952 the sixty-four-year-old York began
to reconsider his attitude when he received several letters,
most of them from the South, suggesting he run for president.
Flattered and intrigued, York took the idea seriously enough
to issue a statement assuring President Truman he would not
oppose the Missourian if he sought another term. Realizing,
however, that he had no real chance for the White House,
York shifted his sights to the Tennessee gubernatorial contest. His latest project was an attempt to secure a junior college for the Fentress County area, and York believed a successful run for the governorship would put him in a stronger
position to achieve his goal. Despite this lure, poor health and
the old reluctance to be away from home eventually persuaded York to stay out of the campaign.[14]

Another of York's postwar activities was an effort to
develop the oil resources of the Cumberland region. At least
as early as 1921, York had begun thinking of the potential
mineral wealth beneath his native mountains, and petroleum
held a particularly strong fascination for him. "He liked the
smell of it," as one of his sons remembered. Now on a firm
financial footing thanks to income from the movie, he spent
some two thousand dollars acquiring a thirty-year-old cable
tool rig and drilling rights to several thousand acres, and on
June 10, 1946, made his first strike approximately six miles
from his Pall Mall home. Encouraged, York persevered until,
a year later, in July 1947, the *Upper Cumberland Times*
headlined, "York Strikes Big Oil Well." The sergeant's
"gusher" delivered fourteen barrels an hour and, at two dollars
a barrel, earned roughly five hundred dollars daily, money that
York planned to divert to his Bible school. The exultant
wildcatter told the Nashville *Banner*, "Shucks, I knew I'd hit
her. It was just a matter of time." Eager for community as
well as personal prosperity, York was active in attracting major oil companies to the mountains for prospecting expedi-
tions. He brought representatives of Standard Oil and other

firms to his site and joined Governor Gordon Browning in a 1949 parade through Nashville highlighting "Oil Progress Week" in Tennessee.[15]

Life magazine told its readers that the Tennessean had "struck it rich," but unfortunately York's oil enterprises did not actually prosper. Like most wildcatters, York found his drilling was usually futile, and what crude oil he did tap was considered of poor quality in those days of cheap and plentiful petroleum. George Edward Buxton York later lamented he would like to have the money his father had sunk in dry holes. By 1959, York's substantial investment yielded him just three hundred dollars a year.[16]

As his business efforts faltered, simultaneously York's health began to fail. He had encountered occasional medical problems since his gall bladder surgery in the mid-1920s, some of which he considered service related. Extending his swollen, aching hands to one 1938 visitor, York recalled the trenches of France as he said, "I think that dampness, days and nights in wet uniforms—mud and more mud—all helped bring this about." In March 1942 he fell acutely ill with lobar pneumonia, and by 1945, with his weight at 250 pounds, high blood pressure was becoming a serious problem for him. Three years later, York suffered the first in a series of strokes. The initial seizure left the right side of his face with a paralysis that "comes and goes," but a more serious stroke in May 1949 threatened his life. Another bout with pneumonia the following year delayed his recovery, and then, in February 1954, a second major stroke left him completely bedfast. Over the next ten years his condition was further complicated by additional medical difficulties related to poor circulation. For example, his eyesight deteriorated steadily, leaving him nearly blind. Now confined to his home almost exclusively, York made his last public appearance in Jamestown in 1957 when the Eighty-second Airborne Association gave him a car with a wheelchair installed in it.[17]

Despite his illness, York remained very much the master of his own house. As one caller noted, "He was completely in charge of the whole operation." He still ordered his wife about in his blunt, affectionate manner, and long after he stopped driving, he kept his car keys in a small purse, permitting no one to take them without his permission. Visited by a photographer from the Nashville *Tennessean*, he waved aside Mrs. York's repeated suggestions that he shave for the portrait and directed the visitor to include a York grandchild in one of his pictures. His gruffness took on a special edge with those who aroused his suspicions. During one well-publicized visit in 1960, a representative of a game company slipped a rook deck into his hands, hoping to get a publicity shot of Sergeant York dealing rook. Noticing the hovering photographer, York dropped the cards to the floor, snapping, "I don't use those."[18]

Although his mind remained clear, York's invalid status brought an end to his long years of public service. He could no longer serve actively on the Fentress County Draft Board and, more disappointingly, his long-planned Bible school collapsed. Its construction delayed because of shortages of materials during the war, York had nevertheless managed to complete one wing and an auditorium, often using volunteer labor that stayed as guests in his home while they worked. Roughly a hundred students attended the school, but after his strokes, York was progressively less able to raise money or oversee its activities, and the institute quickly declined without his ongoing leadership.[19]

The defunct institution played an important role in a ten-year battle between the ailing York and the Internal Revenue Service over alleged nonpayment of taxes, a dispute rooted in the roughly $150,000 he had received in 1942 and 1943 from *Sergeant York*, plus annual royalties derived from showings of the film. Contending that the money should be counted as capital gains rather than income, he had accordingly paid a capital gains tax and then used the rest for the Bible school. "I paid 'em the tax I owed 'em and I don't owe 'em no more," York said. As he summarized it, "When I got that money I paid them [IRS] half and told 'em the other half was mine." In 1951 the IRS rejected the capital gains argument and assessed York $85,422.03 in back income tax and interest, a sum far beyond his ability to pay. With pressure from the government mounting, York adamantly insisted he owed nothing and warned treasury agents, "I've still got the first shotgun I ever owned. And if anybody comes monkeying around here, I'll show him what I can do."[20]

With virtually no cash to counterbalance a mounting stack of debts, York's financial situation was acute by the late 1950s. In 1959 he supported himself, his wife, and an elderly sister-in-law on $3,483.15, a figure that included the meager $10 a month awarded to all retired winners of the Medal of Honor. An IRS audit that year set York's net worth including real estate at roughly $25,000 but put his cash assets at less than $30. Meanwhile, accumulating interest had raised his tax bill to $172,723.10 and he owed an additional $2,700 in medical bills, $5,300 in mortgages, $762 in back real estate taxes, and $600 in notes and small accounts. Faced with this overwhelming debt, his family was deeply concerned that Mrs. York would lose everything if the sergeant died before the tax matter was resolved.[21]

Finally, in early 1961, Speaker of the House Sam Rayburn and Tennessee Congressman Joe Evins came to York's rescue. Evins had long sought a resolution to his constituent's difficulties, while Rayburn took an interest because he had been born in the Cumberland Mountains shortly before his family moved to Texas. The two men acted in response to growing public sympathy for York. As early as 1957, a federal tax court judge had suggested a compromise between the IRS and York, and two years later the Tennessee House of Representatives adopted a resolution asking the government to "go easy" on York. President Dwight Eisenhower received dozens of letters from ordinary citizens across the country asking him to intercede on the sergeant's behalf with the IRS. The Nashville law firm of Hooker and Hooker took on the case without charge and the West Tennessee American Legion began a subscription drive to help York with his taxes. York supporters argued that Congress had given tax breaks on their memoirs to President Truman and President Eisenhower that could just as easily be extended to York's filmed "memoirs."[22]

With the powerful Rayburn now involved, the IRS agreed

to settle for twenty-five thousand dollars, approximately York's net worth. Rayburn and Evins then formed the Help Sergeant York Committee to collect popular donations to pay the tax bill. Rayburn's pledge of a thousand dollars made him the first of some ten thousand Americans to contribute to the fund over a six-week period. A startled Gracie York began receiving shoeboxes of money mailed to her by school children across the country to help meet the twenty-five thousand dollar goal. On April 19, 1961, the committee officially settled York's account with the IRS and placed an additional twenty-five thousand it had received in a trust fund that paid York one hundred dollars a month. Beyond this, Delaware industrialist and philanthropist S. Halleck du Pont created a second trust that paid York another three hundred dollars monthly. Stunned, but "mighty grateful," York told interviewers, "Those tax folks have been a'hounding me so long and I been a'fighting them so long, I just thought it would never end."[23]

York's long struggle with the IRS illustrates the problems his hero status could create for him. Unaccustomed to managing large sums of money, he simply did not know how to handle his windfall in order to minimize his tax payments. Although most writers who dealt with Alvin York neglected such sadder aspects of York's life, at least one person glimpsed the human cost of the sergeant's public acclaim. In 1943 and again in 1959, Pulitzer Prize-winning author Robert Penn Warren published novels featuring characters loosely modeled on Sergeant York. A native of Guthrie, Kentucky, a small town about a hundred miles from Pall Mall, Warren often drew on Kentucky and Tennessee topics in his work. *At Heaven's Gate*, a novel apparently inspired by the politics-and-banking empire of Luke Lea, included a secondary character named Private Porsum, a Tennessee mountaineer who had won the Congressional Medal of Honor in World War I. Writing to Vanderbilt historian Frank Owsley, Warren told his colleague he had checked out every book about York in the Tennessee State Library while creating Private Porsum. Like Sergeant York, Private Porsum was a mountain blacksmith who became a hero by sniping at German machine gunners. A committed Christian who prayed as he fought, Porsum refused even a promotion for his exploit. Porsum differed from York, however, in that Porsum entered the state legislature after returning to Tennessee and eventually became a bank president.[24]

Private Porsum is not Alvin York any more than Willie Stark is Huey Long; nevertheless, through Porsum, Warren provides a commentary on the dilemmas of real-life heroism. A decent, honest man, Porsum was exploited and corrupted by shrewder men eager to use his reputation to advance their own interests. Tortured by the discovery that he had been duped by men he trusted, Porsum lamented that the machine gunners had not shot him in their final volley. In the end he won a measure of redemption when he was killed by a mob while trying to prevent the lynching of a black man.[25]

Sixteen years later, Warren again drew loosely on York to prepare the figure of Jack Herrick in *The Cave*. Warren presented Herrick as the "old heller of high coves and hoot-owl hollers," another rowdy mountain blacksmith who won the Medal of Honor in World War I. Back home in Tennessee after the war, he cultivated his already considerable reputation as a brawler, carouser, and womanizer. However, like Alvin York in 1959, the Jack Herrick of *The Cave* was an aging invalid, the vitality of his youth long since spent. Still pursued by a reputation he could no longer sustain, Herrick tried to find his real self amid the legends of his prodigal past.[26]

With Private Porsum and Jack Herrick, Warren explored the human burden of being a hero. Porsum is a tragic example of a naive man unable to protect himself in the complicated world heroism created for him. While Porsum illustrates the moral frailty of the hero, Jack Herrick, confined to a wheelchair and dying of cancer, illustrates his physical frailty as well. More importantly, Warren developed the family tensions that grew out of Jack's heroism. His older son Jasper grew up intimidated by the pressure of being Jack's son. Although he too became a war hero, his war, Korea, was not so morally neat as World War I, nor did he kill as many men as his father had or receive as high a decoration. He returned to fictional Johntown, Tennessee, as a man still seeking to escape his father and establish his own identity.[27]

Not everything Warren suggested about his characters was also true of Alvin York, but Warren is virtually the only writer to have appreciated the burden York's fame imposed on him. Whereas most writing about York has a positive even saccharine quality to it, Warren's work stresses frailty and mortality. He portrayed his war heroes as men ill equipped to face the challenge of peace and domestic life. Jack Herrick felt himself to be "a dream dreamed up from the weakness of the people." He had become their symbol of violence, strength, and freedom. The real test for such men, Warren said, comes later when they must confront the gap between their legend and their humanity, when they must come to terms with how their lives have changed. Like Private Porsum and Jack Herrick, Alvin York had learned painful lessons about the hidden costs of public adulation.[28]

Despite tax bills and advancing debility, York's life was brightened by periodic tokens of esteem. In May 1960, Fentress County school children staged a play depicting major scenes from his life, a tribute York counted among the most meaningful he ever received. That same year Governor Buford Ellington led a motorcade of dignitaries from Nashville to join American Legion officials in presenting him a push button operated, "ferris wheel" style bed designed to enhance his mobility. "Seems like everything is push button these days," York drawled, "including me." President John F. Kennedy sent a complimentary note with "Good health to you!" scrawled across the bottom in the presidential handwriting. Morever, York continued to observe and comment on public affairs in his usual direct manner. When Secretary of Defense Robert S. MacNamara announced a plan to reduce reserve and National Guard forces, York told reporters, "Nothing would please Khrushchev better." He joined the rest of the nation in acclaiming John Glenn, the first American to orbit the earth, wiring the astronaut, "You have done more to achieve a lasting peace than two presidents have done in the last twenty years.[29]

York's tribute to Glenn may indicate his awareness that he and the pilot of Friendship 7 filled similar places in the public mind. In one sense the two men seem to be very different. York symbolized a world of log cabins and long rifles while Glenn typified the modern technician who manipulated the sophisticated wizardry of the space age. Nevertheless, strong parallels exist between the public personalities of these two apparently disparate figures. For one thing, they each performed their spectacular feats alone, calling up images of the rugged individualism Americans prize so highly. Admittedly Glenn was actually the most visible member of a huge organization that made his flight possible, but press coverage and popular acclaim centered almost exclusively on him. Secondly, Glenn and York openly espoused such traditional values as family, religion, and community. A Presbyterian from a small midwestern town, Glenn toured Washington, New York, and New Concord, Ohio, accompanied by his parents, wife, and children, and, like York in 1919, he seemed to delight more in his return to his hometown than in his ticker tape procession down Broadway. Finally, both Glenn and York appeared to represent the pioneer spirit. To many people, York was the last frontiersman, a living link with those who had settled the land. Simultaneously, Glenn was linked with a new frontier, the frontier of space, which promised to be the challenge for Americans of the future. By far the most famous of the seven Project Mercury astronauts, Glenn stirred such public warmth partly because he represented many of the same values York had symbolized for over forty years to a new generation of Americans.

Besides the praise of notables, York was also buoyed by the constant stream of visitors who stopped at his flag bedecked farmhouse to meet him. Always an outdoorsman, his invalid condition was very difficult for him to accept, especially in the first years after his second stroke. "Because he'd always been used to being active . . . ," Mrs. York explained, "he took it pretty hard." While the company "helped him pass the time away," she said, the constant unannounced intrusions could sometimes be a trial for the rest of the family. Mrs. York collected three books of names, each with roughly two thousand entries in it, signed by the people who came to greet her husband.[30]

Mid-1962 brought a sharp decline in York's already frail health. Suffering acutely, he was hospitalized eleven times over the next two years, often at the point of death, but each time he improved and returned home. Finally, in late August 1964, he sank into a coma and was rushed to Nashville Veteran's Hospital where he died on the morning of September 2 with his wife and children at his bedside. Although Tennessee governor Frank Clement suggested a lying in state at the capitol, the Reverend George Edward Buxton York politely declined the offer, saying, "We think it is best just to take him on back to Jamestown."[31]

The funeral was held in York's Chapel where the sergeant had once taught Sunday School. Roughly eight thousand people jammed Pall Mall for the services, including General Matthew Ridgway, a former commander of the Eighty-second Division representing President Lyndon Johnson. As the last notes of "Onward Christian Soldiers" faded away, the cortege followed his casket up Alvin York Highway to a narrow dirt road leading to the cemetery. The plain ceremony and the simple gravesite were precisely what York had wanted. "I like it here," he once said of the Valley of the Three Forks of the Wolf. "I wouldn't ever like it anywhere else. . . . I was born here and I'll die here. No sir, they won't take me to Arlington. When I die they'll put me away with the rest of the folks in the old family graveyard."[32]

The morning after Alvin York's death, the *New York Times* described him as "the latter day descendant of the American frontier, a plain-talking, no-nonsense sharpshooter who combined in his lanky frame the backwoods world of turkey shoots and corn liquor and the fundamentalist piety of his mountain home." The most common of men, York was a very unlikely hero. He never sought political power or accumulated great wealth or commanded huge armies in battle, the kinds of achievements Americans usually respect most highly. He knew none of the tricks of self-promotion so widely practiced in our media-conscious society. Instead York lived his entire life in an obscure community in the southern Appalachians, largely disdaining money and publicity. Yet from the time he first caught the public imagination in 1919 until his death forty-five years later, York was one of the most popular men in the country.[33]

This adulation he never sought affected York's life profoundly. He was repeatedly thrust into situations which he was ill prepared to handle, and his perplexity was compounded by the fact that society so often praised him for putting aside some of his most cherished values. The man who once refused to kill was told he was a hero when he shot twenty-five men. The man who refused to commercialize his fame was told it was his patriotic duty to permit the filming of *Sergeant York*. Not surprisingly, struggling with such a puzzling world, York made some serious mistakes. For example, his generosity toward educational and religious causes led him into financial trouble, and twice he had to be rescued by public donations. Despite his dedication to the York Institute, he was ineffective as a school administrator and, in the opinion of professional educators, actually retarded the development of the school during the years he served as president and business manager. Moreover, as he grew older, he tragically lost contact with some of the values that had guided his early thinking. Certainly the innocent young pacifist so opposed to killing was very different from the aging national hero who demanded the use of the atomic bomb against his country's enemies.

The wonder is not that York made mistakes, however, but rather that he coped as well as he did with the pressures he faced. If he strayed from some of his early percepts, he nevertheless clung tenaciously to many others. He continued to take a deep pride in his home area even as he worked to improve it, and he never lost his religious-based generosity or commitment to public service. A man who made greatness out of simplicity, he was successful, as few others have been, in the alchemy of turning personal glory into community progress. As the *Times* put it, "one likes to think that the United States was built and protected by such men, simple and pure men who provided the solid foundations on which the more brilliant and imaginative could build."[34]

Notes

1. In The Wolf River Valley

1. William Lynwood Montell, *Don't Go Up Kettle Creek: Verbal Legacy of the Upper Cumberland* (Knoxville: University of Tennessee Press, 1983), 13-15; Robert A. McGaw, "A Likeness of Sergeant York," *Tennessee Historical Quarterly* 27, no. 4 (Winter 1968): 329; Alvin C. York, "Sergeant York's Own Story, A Lecture" (copy in Tennessee State Library and Archives, Nashville, Tennessee). In some sources, the name of the Long Hunter is Pyle.

2. Montell, *Don't Go Up Kettle Creek*, 13-15; Samuel Cowan, *Sergeant York and His People* (New York and London: Funk and Wagnalls, 1922; Grossett and Dunlap, n.d.), 73, 83-96; Albert R. Hogue, *Davy Crockett and Others in Fentress County Who Have Given the County a Prominent Place in History* (Jamestown, Tenn., n.d.), 5, 24-26.

3. York, "Lecture," 3; Cowan, *York*, 120-22, 145; Albert R. Hogue, *History of Fentress County, Tennessee, The Old Home of Mark Twain's Ancestors* (Nashville: Williams Printing Company, 1916), 48.

4. Montell, *Don't Go Up Kettle Creek*, 53-80.

5. Cowan, *York*, 128-31, 135-39; York, "Lecture," 6; Montell, *Don't Go Up Kettle Creek*, 64.

6. Bureau of the Census, *Thirteenth Census of the United States Taken in the Year 1910* (Washington, D.C., 1913), vol. 3, *Population*, 748-49; Cowan, *York*, 11; *Fentress County Gazette*, April 18, 1916; Nashville *Banner*, May 8, 1919.

7. Alvin C. York, "The Other Life as it Was" (manuscript in the possession of the Reverend George Edward Buxton York, Nashville, Tennessee); York, "Lecture," 6-7; McGaw, "Likeness," 329.

8. York, "The Other Life."

9. York, "The Other Life;" York, "Lecture," 6-7; Nashville *Banner*, May 6, 1919.

10. Aelred J. Gray, "Local, State, and Regional Planning," in Thomas R. Ford, ed., *The Southern Appalachian Region: A Survey* (Lexington: Univer-

sity of Kentucky Press, 1962), 169; Cowan *York*, 120-22; York, "The Other Life;" Nashville *Banner*, June 10, 1919.

11. Cowan, *York*, 210; George Pattullo, "The Second Elder Gives Battle," *Saturday Evening Post*, April 26, 1919, 4; York, "Lecture," 7-8; Nashville *Banner*, May 9, 1919.

12. Thomas Skeyhill, ed., *Sergeant York: His Own Life Story and War Diary* (Garden City, N.Y.: Doubleday, Doran, 1928), 129-30; Pattullo, "Second Elder," 3; York, "Lecture," 7; Nashville *Banner*, May 6, 1919.

13. Cowan, *York*, 213; Skeyhill, *Sergeant York*, 134-35; Pattullo, "Second Elder," 3; York, "The Other Life;" Nashville *Banner*, May 6, 1919.

14. Skeyhill, *Sergeant York*, 132-33.

15. *Ibid.*; Cowan, *York*, 151-60; Nashville *Banner*, May 9, 1919.

16. Skeyhill, *Sergeant York*, 131-32; Pattullo, "Second Elder," 4; York, "The Other Life."

17. Mrs. Gracie Williams York, interview with Dr. Joseph H. Riggs, WMC-TV, Memphis, Tennessee, February 28, 1969 (transcript in Memphis Public Library), 7-8; Howard and Betsy Ross York Lowrey (son-in-law and daughter of Alvin C. York), interview with the author and Professor Joseph M. Boggs, June 27, 1978, Bowling Green, Kentucky; Knoxville *Journal and Tribune*, June 15, 1919.

18. G.W. York, interview with Riggs, 2-3; York, "The Other Life;" Knoxville *Journal and Tribune*, June 15, 1919.

19. Pattullo, "Second Elder," 3; York, "Lecture," 7; York, "The Other Life."

20. York, "The Other Life;" Nashville *Banner*, May 7, 1919.

21. Bureau of the Census, *Religious Bodies, 1916* (Washington, D.C., 1919), part 2, *Separate Denominations: History, Description, and Statistics*, 201-4; Elmer T. Clark, *The Small Sects in America*, rev. ed. (New York and Nashville: Abingdon-Cokesbury Press, 1949), 83; H.K. Carroll, *American Church History: The Religious Forces of the United States* (New York: Christian Literature Company, 1893), 99-102.

22. Clark, *Small Sects*, 72-76.

23. Carroll, *Religious Forces*, 99-102.

24. Nashville *Banner*, May 7, 1919; Bureau of the Census, *Religious Bodies, 1916*, 201-4; Carroll, *Religious Forces*, 99-102.

25. Hogue, *History of Fentress County*, 113-14; Nashville *Banner*, May 7, 1919.

26. York, "Lecture," 6.

27. Pattullo, "Second Elder." 3; York, "The Other Life."

2. In the Service of the Lord

1. *Fentress County Gazette*, 1914-16, inclusive.

2. G.W. York, interview with Riggs 2-3, 6, 23; *Fentress County Gazette*, May 25, 1916; Skeyhill, *Sergeant York*, 147-51.

3. Nashville *Banner*, May 7, 1919; Skeyhill, *Sergeant York*, 147.

4. John C. Campbell, *The Southern Highlander and His Homeland* (New York: Russell Sage Foundation, 1921), 120-21.

5. Carroll, *Religious Forces*, 99-102.

6. York, "Lecture," 8; Nashville *Tennessean*, December 15, 1941.

7. Skeyhill, *Sergeant York*, 153-57. York's draft card is in the Federal Archives and Records Center, East Point, Georgia.

8. York, "Lecture," 8.

9. *Ibid.*, 8-10.

10. Skeyhill, *Sergeant York*, 168-74; Pattullo, "Second Elder," 4.

11. Clipping, York Family Scrapbook, 1:25, Tennessee State Library and Archives, Nashville, Tennessee; Skeyhill, *Sergeant York*, 173-77; Pattullo, "Second Elder," 4.

12. Pattullo, "Second Elder," 4; York, "Lecture," 13; Nashville *Banner*, May 6, 1919; Nashville *Tennessean*, June 27, 1941.

13. David M. Kennedy, *Over Here: The First World War and American Society* (New York and Oxford: Oxford University Press, 1980). 163-65.

14. Skeyhill, *Sergeant York*, 177-78.

15. Laurence Stallings, *The Doughboys: The Story of the AEF, 1917-1918* (New York, Evanston, and London: Harper and Row, 1963), 296; Edward Coffman, *The War to End All Wars: The American Military Experience in World War I* (New York: Oxford University Press, 1968), 231, 275-76; Skeyhill, *Sergeant York*, 192.

16. York, "Lecture," 12; Kennedy, *Over Here*, 205.

17. York, "Lecture," 12; Coffman, *War to End All Wars*, 37-38; Skeyhill, *Sergeant York*, 194-95; Harvey DeWeerd, *President Wilson Fights His War* (New York: Macmillan, 1968), 206. The 1917 Enfield was reissued a few weeks later.

18. Russell F. Weigley, *The American Way of War: A History of United States Military Strategy and Policy* (New York: Macmillan, 1973), 202; Coffman, *War to End All Wars*, 126.

19. Coffman, *War to End All Wars*, 273; Stallings, *Doughboys*, 210-11.

20. Skeyhill, *Sergeant York*, 200-201; Stallings, *Doughboys*, 49-52.

21. Skeyhill, *Sergeant York*, 192, 197-98, 202-3, 209-10; York, "Lecture," 13-14.

22. Coffman, *War to End All Wars*, 125-216.

23. Skeyhill, *Sergeant York*, 205-6; Stallings, *Doughboys*, 202.

24. Skeyhill, *Sergeant York*, 195, 207-10; York, "Lecture," 13-14.

3. The Shadow of Death

1. Stallings, *Doughboys*, 224.

2. *Ibid.*, 224-26; Robert Leckie, *The Wars of America* (New York, Evanston, and London: Harper and Row, 1968), 652; Frank Vandiver, *Black Jack: The Life and Times of John J. Pershing* (College Station, Tex., and London: Texas A & M Press,1977), 2:940.

3. Skeyhill, *Sergeant York*, 211-12; George Duncan, "Reminiscences of

the World War" (unpublished memoir, University of Kentucky, Lexington, Kentucky); Coffman, *War to End All Wars*, 215.

4. Stallings, *Doughboys*, 228-31, 236-48.

5. *Ibid.*, 296; Coffman, *War to End All Wars*, 323-24; Duncan, "Reminiscences," 120-21, 146-47; Divisional Officers, *Official History of 82nd Division, American Expeditionary Forces, 1917-1919* (Indianapolis: Bobbs-Merrill, 1920), 37.

6. Duncan, "Reminiscences," 146; Coffman, *War to End All Wars*, 324-26.

7. Duncan, "Reminiscences," 150; Skeyhill, *Sergeant York*, 217-19.

8. Coffman, *War to End All Wars*, 323-24.

9. Field Order No. 2, 164th Infantry Brigade File, Box 15, 82nd Division Historical Records, Record Group 120, National Archives, Washington, D.C.; Skeyhill, *Sergeant York*, 217-19, 237-38.

10. Divisional Officers, *Official History*, 56-62; Skeyhill, *Sergeant York*, 238.

11. "The Origin of War Legends: An Investigation of the Alleged Feat of Sergeant York, October 8, 1918" (Reichsarchiv) 1929, translation in the records of the Army War College, Thomas File, Record Group 165, National Archives, Washington, D.C.

12. *Ibid.*, 9-10, 20; U.S. Department of War, *Histories of Two Hundred and Fifty-One Divisions of the German Army Which Participated in the War (1914-1918)* (Washington, 1920), 62-63, 464-67.

13. "Origin of War Legends," 9-10.

14. Skeyhill, *Sergeant York*, 238; Stallings, *Doughboys*, 297.

15. Skeyhill, *Sergeant York*, 225, 238, 241-44; Stallings, *Doughboys*, 298; Nat Brandt, "Sergeant York," *American Heritage* 35, no. 2 (August/September 1981): 61. The number of squads detailed to Early is unclear. Parsons says he sent four squads, but other participants in the fight say he sent only three. I have concluded three is the correct number because all the men except Early belonged to the squads led by Cutting, Savage, or York. The fate of the two Germans with Red Cross arm bands is also uncertain. York said they both ran away, but other doughboys say one of them was captured. I have accepted the latter view because most members of the patrol attested to it in their affidavits. See Skeyhill, *Sergeant York*, 236-69.

16. "Origin of War Legends," 16-18.

17. *Ibid.*, 12, 14, 16-19.

18. *Ibid.*, 16-19; Skeyhill, *Sergeant York*, 225, 238, 241-44; Stallings, *Doughboys*, 299-300; Brandt, "Sergeant York," 61-62.

19. Skeyhill, *Sergeant York*, 226, 231, 264, 271; Stallings, *Doughboys*, 299-300; Brandt, "Sergeant York," 61-62; Divisional Officers, *Official History*, 61-62. According to its official history, the Eighty-second was equipped with the 1917 Enfield (Eddystone) rifle. Presumably York was using such a weapon.

20. Skeyhill, *Sergeant York*, 251; Stallings, *Doughboys*, 300; Pattullo, "Second Elder," 73; Brandt, "Sergeant York," 61-62; Divisional Officers, *Official History*, 61-62.

21. York, "Lecture," 18-19; Skeyhill, *Sergeant York,* 253, 265-66; Brandt, "Sergeant York," 62-63.

22. "Origin of War Legends," 9, 16, 18; Brandt, "Sergeant York," 63.

23. Stallings, *Doughboys,* 300-301; York, "Lecture," 19; Cowan, *York,* 64, 209-10; Pattullo, "Second Elder," 74; Brandt, "Sergeant York," 63.

24. "Origin of War Legends," 20-21; York, "Lecture," 19-20; Brandt, "Sergeant York," 63.

25. "Origin of War Legends," 13-16.

26. *Ibid.*, 8-9; Pattullo, "Second Elder," 74; Brandt, "Sergeant York," 63.

27. Pattullo, "Second Elder," 74.

28. Duncan, "Reminiscences," 150; York, "Lecture," 20; Stallings, *Doughboys,* 300; Henry Swindler, "York of Tennessee," 1, 8, records of the Army War College, Thomas File, RG 165.

29. Cowan, *York,* 75, "Lecture," 25; *Senate Calendar No. 536, Report 506,* "Sergeant Alvin C. York" 68th Cong., 1st sess.; Swindler, "York of Tennessee," 8.

30. Henry Swindler to George Edward Bruxton [*sic*], July 17, 1929; Swindler to Edward Danforth, July 29, 1929, records of the Army War College, Thomas File, RG 165.

31. Swindler, "York of Tennessee;" Skeyhill, *Sergeant York,* 236-78.

32. "Origin of War Legends," 1-5, 12, 25-26.

33. *Ibid.*, 8, 13, 22-23.

34. *Ibid.*, 19, 23-24.

35. *Ibid.*, 2, 12, 19, 23-24.

36. *Ibid.*, 5-8, 12-16, 20-21, 24; Lt. Col. Richard Wetherill to Maj. Gen. George Duncan, November 8, 1918; "Personnel," 164th Infantry Brigade Organizational Records, Box 438, RG 120.

37. "Origin of War Legends," 22-24.

38. *Ibid.*, 13, 22; Edward Danforth to Henry Swindler, August 5, 1929, records of the Army War College, Thomas File, RG 165; Divisional Officers, *Official History,* 57-58.

39. *New York Times,* May 22, 1919; October 7, 1929; August 11, 13, 1935. At least one other member of the patrol, Corporal William Cutting, also believed his contributions had been slighted. A mysterious fellow who had enlisted under an assumed name (his real name was Otis B. Merrithew), Cutting was wounded in the left arm by the same salvo that struck Early, yet he insisted he had returned fire using his pistol. Contending that he rather than York was actually in command after Early went down, Cutting claimed equal credit for leading the prisoners back to American lines. Cutting was still hospitalized when Buxton conducted his investigation, and he felt his role was therefore lost. Buxton himself was genuinely uncertain about Cutting's contribution, although he never doubted York's story. Regarding Cutting, York told Buxton he was so busy in the firefight that he had no idea what the others were doing. Cutting complained to Buxton for years, but he never received satisfaction. See Buxton to Duncan, April 22, 1932, in George Duncan Scrapbook, Special Collections, Univ. of Kentucky Library.

40. *New York Times*, August 11, 13, 1935; Swindler, "York of Tennessee," 8-10; Brandt, "Sergeant York," 63-64.

41. Duncan, "Reminiscences," 125, 144; Skeyhill, *Sergeant York*, 239.

42. "Origin of War Legends," 22-24.

43. Skeyhill, *Sergeant York*, 270-72; Pattullo, "Second Elder," 74; George Edward Buxton York, interview with the author and Professor Joseph M. Boggs, July 12, 1978, Nashville, Tennessee.

44. Pattullo, "Second Elder," 3, 73-74; Skeyhill, *Sergeant York*, 278.

45. Skeyhill, *Sergeant York*, 281; York, "Lecture," 23.

4. An American Hero

1. Dixon Wecter, *The Hero in America: A Chronicle of Hero Worship* (New York: Charles Scribner's Sons, 1941; reissued, 1972), xiv, 1; Samuel P. Hays, *The Response to Industrialism, 1885-1914* (Chicago, Univ. of Chicago Press, 1957); Robert Wiebe, *The Search for Order, 1877-1920* (New York: Hill and Wang, 1967).

2. Coffman, *War to End All Wars*, 38; Leckie, *Wars of America*, 608-9; Skeyhill, *Sergeant York*, vii.

3. William Leuchtenburg, *The Perils of Prosperity, 1914-1932* (Chicago: University of Chicago Press, 1958); Robert Murray, *The Red Scare* (Minneapolis: University of Minnesota Press, 1955).

4. Stallings, *Doughboys*, 1-2; Skeyhill, *Sergeant York*, 285-86; Duncan, "Reminiscences," 172.

5. York Family Scrapbook, 1:46; Skeyhill, *Sergeant York*, 289-91.

6. Morris Goldman to John J. Pershing, November 22, 1921; Pershing to Goldman, December 3, 1921, John J. Pershing Papers, Library of Congress, Washington, D.C.; Robert McGaw to Sam Smith, et al., February 20, 1968, York State Committee File, Alvin York Papers, Tennessee State Library and Archives, Nashville, Tennessee; *New York Times*, March 22, 1931; Skeyhill, *Sergeant York*, 292; McGaw, "Likeness," 330.

7. Goldman to Pershing, November 22, 1921; Pershing to Goldman, December 3, 1921, Pershing Papers.

8. Skeyhill, *Sergeant York*, 292; McGaw, "Likeness," 330.

9. Frank L. Mott, *A History of American Magazines, 1885-1905* (Cambridge, Mass.: Belknap Press, 1957), 4:688, 694, 696; James Playsted Wood, *Magazines in the United States*, 2nd ed. (New York: Ronald Press Company, 1956), 154-55; James Playsted Wood, *The Curtis Magazines* (New York: Ronald Press Company, 1971), 86-88.

10. George Pattullo to Westbrook Pegler, January 17, 1958, Westbrook Pegler Papers, Herbert Hoover Presidential Library, West Branch, Iowa.

11. *Ibid.*; Pattullo, "Second Elder," 3-4, 71-74; Knoxville *Journal and Tribune*, June 15, 1919.

12. Pattullo, "Second Elder," 3-4, 71-74.

13. Henry Shapiro, *Appalachia on Our Mind: The Southern Mountains and Mountaineers in the American Consciousness, 1870-1920* (Chapel Hill:

University of North Carolina Press, 1977), ix-xx, 252; Henry Shapiro, "Appalachia and the Idea of America," in J.W. Williamson, ed., *An Appalachian Symposium: Essays Written in Honor of Cratis D. Williams* (Boone, N.C.: Appalachian Consortium Press, 1977), 43-46.

14. Pattullo, "Second Elder," 3-4, 71-74.

15. Shapiro, *Appalachia on Our Mind*, ix-xix, 256-65.

16. *Ibid.*, 262-64.

17. Robert Bellah, "Civil Religion in America," *Daedalus* 96, no. 1 (Winter 1967): 1-21.

18. *Ibid.*

19. Cowan, *York*, 268-71; Nashville *Banner*, May 6-9, 12, 1919.

20. Skeyhill, *Sergeant York*, 295-97; Clipping, York Family Scrapbook, 1:17; *New York Times*, May 23, 1919.

21. H. and B.R.Y. Lowrey, interview with the author and Boggs; Skeyhill, *Sergeant York*, 297-98.

22. H. and B.R.Y. Lowrey, interview with the author and Boggs; Clipping, York Family Scrapbook, 1:21; *Congressional Record*, 66th Cong., 1st sess., 199; *New York Times*, May 25, 1919; Cowan, *York*, 50; Skeyhill, *Sergeant York*, 298-99.

23. Clipping, York Family Scrapbook, 1:22-23; *New York Times*, May 30, 1919; Cowan, *York*, 271-72.

24. Clippings, York Family Scrapbook, 1:22-25; *New York Times*, June 1, 1919.

25. Clippings, York Family Scrapbook 1:25-27; Nashville *Banner*, June 9, 1919.

26. Nashville *Banner*, June 10-11, 1919.

27. Nashville *Banner*, June 10-14, 1919.

28. Clippings, York Family Scrapbook, 1:21, 46; 2:n.p.; *New York Times*, January 26, 1922; Skeyhill, *Sergeant York*, 299-300.

29. Skeyhill, *Sergeant York*, 299-300; York, "Lecture," 25; G.E.B. York, interview with the author and Boggs.

30. Nashville *Banner*, June 10-11, 1919.

31. Clippings, York Family Scrapbook, 1:7-16; 2:n.p.; Nashville *Banner*, May 6-7, 1919.

32. Clippings, York Family Scrapbook, 1:26, 27, 29; Nashville *Banner*, June 10-11, 1919; July 24, 1928; September 2, 1964; Nashville *Tennessean*, July 24, 1926; Bolivar *Bulletin*, July 23, 1926; Selmer, *McNairy County Independent*, July 30, 1926.

33. Dixon Wecter, *When Johnny Comes Marching Home* (Cambridge, Mass.: Houghton-Mifflin, 1944), 328; Richard Ernest Dupuy, *A Compact History of the United States Army*, rev. ed. (New York and London: Hawthorne Books, 1961), 227; Vandiver, *Black Jack*, 2:969, 977; Stallings, *Doughboys*, 335-38; *New York Times*, March 22, 1931; September 3, 1964.

34. Kennedy, *Over Here*, v-vii, 144-90; Marcus Cunliffe, *Soldiers and Civilians: The Martial Spirit in America, 1775-1865* (Boston and Toronto: Little, Brown and Company, 1968).

35. Skeyhill, *Sergeant York*, vii.

36. Kennedy, *Over Here*, v-vii, 146-53; John William Ward, "The Meaning of Lindbergh's Flight," *American Quarterly* 10 (Spring 1958): 3-16.

37. Ward, "Lindbergh's Flight," 3-16.

5. The Hero at Home

1. Skeyhill, *Sergeant York*, 303-5.

2. *Ibid.*; New York *World*, December 4, 1921, clipping in York Family Scrapbook, 2:n.p.

3. Montell, *Don't Go Up Kettle Creek*, 51.

4. New York *World*, December 4, 1921, clipping in York Family Scrapbook, 2:n.p.

5. Nashville *Banner* clippings, York Family Scrapbook, 2:n.d., n.p.

6. Chicago *Tribune*, December 9, 1921, clipping in York Family Scrapbook, 2:n.p.; Wecter, *When Johnny Comes Marching Home*, 327-29; Stallings, *Doughboys*, 335-38.

7. New York *World*, December 4, 1921, clipping in York Family Scrapbook, 2:n.p.; Nashville *Banner* clippings, York Family Scrapbook, 2:n.d., n.p.

8. New York *World*, December 4, 1921, clipping in York Family Scrapbook, 2:n.p.

9. *Ibid.*; Chicago *Tribune*, December 9, 1921, clipping in York Family Scrapbook, 2:n.p.

10. New York *World*, December 4, 1921, clipping in York Family Scrapbook, 2:n.p.; Skeyhill, *Sergeant York*, 306.

11. New York *World*, December 4, 1921, clipping in York Family Scrapbook, 2:n.p.; Bureau of the Census, *Thirteenth Census*, vol. 3, *Population*, 717-21, 748-49; Skeyhill, *Sergeant York*, 308; Wecter, *When Johnny Comes Marching Home*, 269; David D. Lee, *Tennessee in Turmoil: Politics in the Volunteer State, 1920-1932* (Memphis: Memphis State University Press, 1979), 7.

12. New York *World*, December 4, 1921, clipping in York Family Scrapbook, 2:n.p.; *New York Times*, June 6, 1926; June 19, 1927; Cowan *York*, 288-89.

13. New York *World*, December 4, 1921, clipping in York Family Scrapbook, 2:n.p.; *New York Times*, June 6, 1926; June 19, 1927; Andrew Jackson York, interview with the author and Professor Joseph Mason Boggs, July 1, 1978, Pall Mall, Tennessee; G.E.B. York, interview with the author and Boggs.

14. *The Mountaineer* (April 1926); pamphlets in Alvin York file, Pershing Papers.

15. Mrs. Arthur S. Bushing, Sr., and Arthur S. Bushing, Jr., interview with the author, July 11, 1978, Maryville, Tennessee; Skeyhill, *Sergeant York*, 10-11.

16. Nashville *Tennessean*, April 8, 10, 1925; *Tennessee House Journal, 1925* (Nashville, 1925), 1195, 1254; *Tennessee Senate Journal, 1925* (Nashville, 1925), 1194.

17. *Private Acts of the State of Tennessee Passed by the Sixty-fourth General Assembly, 1925* (Nashville, 1925), 2:2866-74.

18. Mrs. A.S. Bushing, Sr., and A.S. Bushing, Jr., interview with the author.

19. Alvin York to Austin Peay, et al., March 11, 1926; W.I. Jones to Austin Peay, April 17, 1926, Austin Peay Official Papers, Box 25, File 8, Tennessee State Library and Archives, Nashville, Tennessee; York to Peay, September 30, 1924, Austin Peay Family Papers, Folder 28, Tennessee State Library and Archives; W.A. Garrett to Perry L. Harned and the Tennessee State Board of Education, July 15, 1929, papers of the Tennessee State Board of Education, unsorted, Tennessee State Library and Archives; *New York Times*, March 17, 1926.

20. *Private Acts of the State of Tennessee Passed by the Sixty-fifth General Assembly, 1927* (Nashville, 1927), 1:411-16; Nashville *Tennessean*, January 27, 1927; *New York Times*, July 26, 1927.

21. W.A. Garrett to Perry L. Harned and the Tennessee State Board of Education, July 15, 1929, papers of the Tennessee State Board of Education, unsorted.

22. *Mountain Courier*, November 13, 1931.

23. *Fentress County News*, December 8, 1927; Knoxville *Journal*, September 17, 1927; Nashville *Tennessean*, September 16, 1926; *New York Times*, September 17, 18, 1927.

24. Lee, *Tennessee in Turmoil*, 19-75; Joseph T. Macpherson, "Democratic Progressivism in Tennessee: The Administrations of Austin Peay" (Ph.D. diss., Vanderbilit, 1969), 349-81.

25. Lee, *Tennessee in Turmoil*, 10-12.

26. Austin Peay to W.I. Jones, April 22, 1926; Alvin York to Peay, April 24, 1926; Peay to York, May 8, 1926, Peay Official Papers, Box 25, File 8.

27. Alvin York to Austin Peay, June 3, 1926, Peay Family Papers, Folder 28; Lee, *Tennessee in Turmoil*, 63-76, 183-84; Shirley Hassler, comp., *Fifty Years of Tennessee Primaries, 1916-1966* (Nashville: State of Tennessee, 1967), 131; Shirley Hassler, comp., *Fifty Years of Tennessee Elections, 1916-1966* (Nashville: State of Tennessee, 1967), 103. Although Fentress County is actually on the edge of Middle Tennessee, its mountainous terrain and Republican politics tied it more closely to East Tennessee.

28. Lee, *Tennessee in Turmoil*, 76-100.

29. Jack Corn (Nashville *Tennessean* photographer), interview with the author and Professor Joseph M. Boggs, July 7, 1978, Bowling Green, Kentucky; Chattanooga *Times*, July 25, 1928; Knoxville *Journal*, July 24, 1928; Nashville *Banner*, July 24, 1928.

30. Lee, *Tennessee in Turmoil*, 97-100, 185; Hassler, *Tennessee Primaries*, 126-27; Hassler, *Tennessee Elections*, 99.

31. Alvin York to Henry Horton, September 17, 1928; Perry L. Harned to York, September 19, 1928, Henry Horton Official Papers, Box 53, File 5, Tennessee State Library and Archives, Nashville, Tennessee.

32. Alvin York to Henry Horton, September 17, 1928; York to Chairman, Finance, Ways, and Means Committee, n.d., 1929; Luke Lea to Horton, April

30, 1929; W.A. Beaty to Horton, August 11, 1929, Horton Official Papers, Box 53, File 5; *Fentress County News*, August 15, 1929.

33. H.N. Wright to Fentress County justices of peace, October 17, 1929; Perry L. Harned to State Board of Education, October 19, 1929, Horton Official Papers, Box 53, File 5; *Fentress County News*, December 5, 1929; Knoxville *Journal*, August 15, 1929.

34. Maude Holman to Alvin York, August 25, 1933, papers of the Tennessee State Board of Education, Box 626, "York Transportation bids;" *Mountain Courier*, November 13, 1931; *Time*, May 25, 1936; H. and B.R.Y. Lowrey, interview with the author and Boggs.

35. *Christian Science Monitor*, March 14, 1942; H. and B.R.Y. Lowrey, interview with the author and Boggs; Mrs. A.S. Bushing, Sr. and A.S. Bushing, Jr., interview with the author; G.E.B. York, interview with the author and Boggs.

36. Alvin York to Cordell Hull, April 6, 11, 1920, Container 2; York to Hull, February 11, 1925, Container 8, Cordell Hull Papers, Library of Congress, Washington, D.C.; Edwin Watson to Franklin D. Roosevelt, May 29, 1939; Harry Woodring to Watson, June 7, 1939; Watson to Roosevelt, June 14, 1939; clerical reminder to Watson, June 16, 1939, Franklin D. Roosevelt Papers, President's Official File, 3695, "Sergeant Alvin C. York," Franklin D. Roosevelt Presidential Library, Hyde Park, New York; *New York Times*, August 6, 1921.

37. Bruce R. Payne to Harold Phelps Stokes, December 29, 1925, Herbert Hoover Papers, Commerce Papers, Box 718, Herbert Hoover Presidential Library, West Branch, Iowa.

38. "Report of the Fact-Finding Committee, Alvin C. York Agricultural Institute" (minutes of the State Board of Education), November 10, 1933, papers of the State Board of Education, unsorted.

39. "York Response to the Fact-Finding Committee," February 1, 1934, Hill McAlister Official Papers, Box 84, File 16, Tennessee State Library and Archives, Nashville, Tennessee.

40. Alvin York to Hill McAlister, September 16, 1935, McAlister Papers, Box 84, File 16; minutes of the State Board of Education, May 8, 1936, papers of the State Board of Education, unsorted.

41. Minutes of the State Board of Education, May 8, 1936, papers of the State Board of Education, unsorted; Alvin York to Walter D. Cocking, May 12, 1936, papers of the State Board of Education, Box 626, "Alvin C. York Agricultural Institute;" *Time*, May 25, 1936; Nashville *Tennessean*, May 9, July 15, 1936; *New York Yimes*, May 9, July 16, 1936.

42. Paul B. Stephens to Henry Burke, January 7, 1938; Albert Hogue to Gordon Browning, January 14, 1938; John T. Peeler to Browning, January 19, 1938; Browning to Peeler, January 24, 1938; Browning to Burke, January 24, 1938; Burke to Browning, February 1, 1938; Alvin York to Stephens, February 28, 1938; Stephens to Browning, February 28, 1938; "Report and Recommendations for Alvin York Agricultural Institute to State Board," submitted by Paul B. Stephens, April 28, 1938, Gordon Browning Official Papers,

Box 20, File 9, Tennessee State Library and Archives, Nashville, Tennessee; J.M. Smith to York, May 9, 1938, papers of the State Board of Education, Box 657.

43. Alvin York to Prentice Cooper, June 5, 1939; minutes of the State Board of Education, August 11, 1939, papers of the State Board of Education, unsorted; Nashville *Banner*, August 11, 31, 1939; Nashville *Tennessean*, August 11, 12, 1939.

44. Nashville *Tennessean*, May 9, 1936.

6. The Legend Makers

1. *Who Was Who Among North American Authors, 1921-1939* (Detroit, 1976); *New York Times*, May 17, 1959.

2. Cowan, *York*, 69-106; *Nation*, July 5, 1922; *New York Times*, July 5, 1922.

3. Skeyhill, *Sergeant York*, 2-4; *New York Times*, May 23, 1932.

4. Skeyhill, *Sergeant York*, 26-29.

5. Mrs. A.S. Bushing, Sr., and A. S. Bushing, Jr., interview with the author.

6. *Ibid.*; Skeyhill, *Sergeant York*, 31-32.

7. Skeyhill, *Sergeant York*, 24-33.

8. *Ibid.*, 58.

9. James S. Metcalfe, "Never to Fight Overseas" (unpublished manuscript, Alvin C. York File, Nashville *Banner* Library, Nashville, Tennessee); *New York Times*, November 11, 1934.

10. *New York Times*, November 11, 1932; November 12, 1937; October 9, 1938.

11. Hector Arce, *Gary Cooper: An Intimate Biography* (New York: William Morrow and Company, 1979), 169-70; Philip Frend, *The Movie Moguls: An Informal History of the Hollywood Tycoons* (Chicago: Henry Regney, 1969), 145-46; Jesse Lasky with Don Weldon, *I Blow My Own Horn* (Garden City, N.Y.: Doubleday and Company, 1957), 252-53; Frances Marion, *Off with Their Heads: A Serio-Comic Tale of Hollywood* (New York: Macmillan, 1972), 8; Larry Swindell, *The Last Hero: A Biography of Gary Cooper* (Garden City, N.Y.: Doubleday and Company, 1980), 232; Norman Zierold, *The Moguls* (New York: Coward-McCanny, 1969), 163-64; Nashville *Tennessean*, September 8, 1940; *New York Times*, June 29, 1941.

12. Arce, *Cooper*, 170; Lasky, *Horn*, 253; Nashville *Banner*, August 3, 1939.

13. Nashville *Tennessean*, March 10, 11, 14, 1940.

14. Lasky, *Horn*, 254-56; Nashville *Tennessean*, March 15, 17, 24, 1940; *New York Times*, March 16, 24, 1940; *Variety*, March 27, 1940.

15. Nashville *Tennessean*, March 15, 24, April 20, 1940; *New York Times* March 16, 1940; *Variety*, March 27, 1940.

16. Nashville *Tennessean*, March 16, 1940.

17. Arce, *Cooper*, 171-75; Lasky, *Horn*, 257-58; Swindell, *Last Hero*, 232-33.

18. Arce, *Cooper*, 171; Lasky, *Horn*, 257; Nashville *Tennessean*, March 24, April 5, 1940.

19. Gary Cooper as told to George Scullin, "Well, It Was This Way," *Saturday Evening Post*, April 7, 1956, 120.

20. *Ibid*.; Rene Jordan, *Gary Cooper, A Pyramid Illustrated History of the Movies* (New York: Pyramid, 1974), 92-94; Peter Bogdanovich, *The Cinema of Howard Hawks* (New York: Film Library of the Museum of Modern Art, 1962), 20-22; Lasky, *Horn*, 259-60; H. and B.R.Y. Lowrey, interview with the author and Boggs.

21. Lasky, *Horn*, 259; Nashville *Banner*, January 10, 1941; Nashville *Tennessean*, July 5, 1941; *New York Times*, February 16, 1941.

22. Arce, *Cooper*, 176; Lasky, *Horn*, 260; Nashville *Tennessean*, April 22, 25, 27, 28, 1940.

23. Arce, *Cooper*, 172-73; Cooper and Scullin, "It Was This Way," 120; Bogdanovich, *Cinema of Hawks*, 20; Nashville *Tennessean*, February 10, June 29, 1941.

24. Samuel Rosenman, comp., *The Public Papers and Addresses of Franklin D. Roosevelt: The Call to Battle Stations* (New York: Harper and Brothers, 1950), 485-87; *New York Times*, January 7, May 18, May 31, November 12, 1941.

25. *New York Times*, July 2-4, 1941.

26. Nashville *Tennessean*, July 3, 1941; *New York Times*, July 3, 1941.

27. Nashville *Tennessean*, July 31, 1941; *New York Times*, July 31, 1941; Mrs. A.S. Bushing, Sr., and A.S. Bushing, Jr., interview with the author.

28. *Congressional Record*, 77th Cong., 1st sess., 6411; *Life*, August 26, 1941; *Time*, August 4, 1941; *Variety*, July 2, 1941.

29. Otis Ferguson, "In the Army Aren't We All," *New Republic*, September 29, 1941, 403-4; *New York Times*, August 2, 1941; *Variety*, August 6, 1941.

30. Nashville *Tennessean*, July 4, 7, 1941; *New York Times*, July 3, 1941.

31. Mrs. Gracie Williams York, interview with the author and Boggs, July 1, 1978, Pall Mall, Tennessee; Nashville *Tennessean*, September 14, 18, 1941; *New York Times*, July 4, 1941.

32. G.W. York, interview with Riggs, 7-8; *Time*, September 11, 1964; Arce, *Cooper*, 176.

33. Robin Wood, *Howard Hawks*, (Garden City, N.Y.: Doubleday and Company, 1968), 165; Andrew Sarris, "The World of Howard Hawks," in Joseph McBride, ed., *Focus on Howard Hawks* (Englewood Cliffs, N.J.: Prentice-Hall, 1972), 49; Cooper and Scullin, "It Was This Way," 120; *Variety*, July 23, 1941.

34. Wood, *Hawks*, 165; Sarris, "World of Hawks," 49; Coffman, *War to End All Wars*, 363; Bogdanovich, *Cinema of Hawks*, 22.

35. Bogdanovich, *Cinema of Hawks*, 22.

36. A.J. York, interview with the author and Boggs.

7. Last Years

1. *Life*, May 11, 1942; *Time*, May 18, 1942; Nashville *Banner*, September 2, 1964; Nashville *Tennessean*, April 24, 28, 1942; *New York Times*, April 28, May 3, 1942.

2. Hugh Walker (Nashville *Tennessean* reporter), interview with the author and Professor Joseph M. Boggs, October 14, 1978, Nashville, Tennessee; G.W. York, interview with the author and Boggs; A.J. York, interview with the author and Boggs; Mrs. A.S. Bushing, Sr., and A.S. Bushing, Jr., interview with the author; *New York Times*, November 19, 1942; August 15, 1948; *Newsweek*, May 18, 1942.

3. Virgil V. Easley to Alvin York, July 31, 1946; York to Harry S. Truman, August 1, 1946; William Hassett to York, August 13, 1946; York to Truman, June 27, 1945; Hassett to York, July 4, 1945, Papers of Harry S. Truman, Official File, Harry S. Truman Presidential Library, Independence, Missouri.

4. G.W. York, interview with Riggs, 12-13; Alvin York to Douglas MacArthur, April 3, 1942; MacArthur to York, April 6, 1942, Franklin D. Roosevelt, Papers, Official File; Nashville *Banner*, February 24, 1942; Nashville *Tennessean*, May 10, 1942; David Lilienthal, *The Journals of David Lilienthal: The TVA Years, 1939-1945* (New York, Evanston, and London: Harper and Row, 1964), 1:446.

5. Omar N. Bradley and Clay Blair, *A General's Life* (New York: Simon and Schuster, 1983), 107; Matthew B. Ridgway, *Soldier: The Memoirs of Matthew B. Ridgway* (New York: Harper and Brothers, 1956), 51-53. At the time of York's visit, the Eighty-second was not yet an airborne unit.

6. H. and B.R.Y. Lowrey, interview with the author and Boggs; Nashville *Banner*, May 13, 1942; Nashville *Tennessean*, May 9, 1936; March 14, 20, 21, 1940; *New York Times*, May 13, 1942.

7. Audie Murphy, *To Hell and Back* (New York: Henry Holt 1949); *New York Times*, June 1, 1971.

8. *New York Times*, June 1, 1971.

9. *New York Times*, March 10, 1949; June 1, 1971; *Saturday Review*, March 26, 1949; New York *Herald Tribune*, February 27, 1949.

10. Murphy, *To Hell and Back*, 273.

11. *Ibid.*, 271-74; Metcalfe, "Never to Fight Overseas," York File.

12. *New York Times*, August 15, 1948; September 3, 1964; *Upper Cumberland Times*, December 4, 1947.

13. William D. Hassett to Alvin York, December 12, 1950, Papers of Harry S. Truman, Official File; Nashville *Tennessean*, July 23, 1950; November 17-18, 1951; March 6, 1952.

14. A.J. York, interview with the author and Boggs; Nashville *Tennessean*, November 17, 1951; *New York Times*, August 15, 1948.

15. Clippings, York Family Scrapbook, 2:n.p.; A.J. York, interview with the author and Boggs; *Life*, August 18, 1947; Nashville *Banner*, July 26-27, 1947; October 20, 1949; *Upper Cumberland Times*, June 27, August 22, 1946; July 24, 31, 1947.

16. G.E.B. York, interview with the author and Boggs; *Life*, August 18, 1947; *New York Times*, April 22, 1961.

17. G.W. York, interview with Riggs, 32; Metcalfe, "Never to Fight Overseas," York File; Nashville *Banner*, May 9, 1949; Nashville *Tennessean*, May 15, 1942; *New York Times*, July 3, 1950; February 28, March 10, 1954; August 22, 1957; September 3, 1964.

18. Corn, interview with the author and Boggs; Walker, interview with the author and Boggs.

19. G.E.B. York, interview with the author and Boggs; *New York Times*, August 15, 1948.

20. H. and B.R.Y. Lowrey, interview with the author and Boggs; *New York Times*, May 3, 1955; September 8, 1960; September 3, 1964; *Newsweek*, October 28, 1957.

21. G.E.B. York, interview with the author and Boggs; *New York Times*, December 31, 1955; April 22, 1961.

22. G.E.B. York, interview with the author and Boggs; *New York Times*, November 19, 1957; February 18, 1959; September 8, 1960; Martin M. Teasley (acting director, Dwight D. Eisenhower Library) to the author, August 5, 1980. See also Ralph A. Dungan to Sally B. Arnold, February 8, 1961, and Dean Barron to Charles Shaw, n.d., John F. Kennedy Papers, WHCS F, pp. 6-21 ST 42, Box 714, John F. Kennedy Presidential Library, Boston, Massachusetts.

23. G.E.B. York, interview with the author and Boggs; *New York Times*, March 19, April 9, 10, 20, 22, May 26, 1961; September 3, 1964.

24. Robert Penn Warren, *At Heaven's Gate* (New York: Random House, 1943); *The Cave* (New York: Random House, 1959); Charles Bohner, *Robert Penn Warren* (New York: Twayne, 1964), 146-48; Robert Penn Warren to Frank Owsley, November 13, 1939, Frank Owsley Papers, Vanderbilt University, Nashville, Tennessee; Daniel Joseph Singal, *The War Within: From Victorian to Modernist Thought in the South, 1919-1945* (Chapel Hill, N.C.: University of North Carolina Press, 1982), 358.

25. Warren, *At Heaven's Gate.*

26. Warren, *The Cave.*

27. *Ibid.*

28. *Ibid.,* 388.

29. John F. Kennedy to Alvin York, February 4, 1961, John F. Kennedy Papers, WHCN F, Box 3091; Nashville *Banner*, September 2, 1964; *New York Times*, October 9, 1960; September 3, 1964.

30. G.W. York, interview with Riggs, 20-21.

31. *New York Times*, September 3, 1964; Chicago *Sun-Times*, September 3, 1964, quoted in *Congressional Record*, 88th Cong., 1st sess., 22188. To the very end of his life, York was deeply devoted to his wife and children. Married to Gracie Williams York for forty-five years, he was fond of saying "The Lord provides everyone with Grace. The Lord has already provided me with mine." The eight York children were Alvin, Jr., (1921-83), a farmer; George Edward Buxton (1923-   ), a minister; Woodrow Wilson (1925-   ), a sawmill worker; Sam Houston (1928-29); Andrew Jackson (1930-   ), a state

park ranger; Betsy Ross (1933-), a secretary; Mary Alice (1935-); a businesswoman; and Thomas Jefferson (1938-72) a state park ranger. York's comment about his wife appears in the Nashville *Banner*, September 4, 1964. I am indebted to Betsy York Lowrey for information about her brothers and sister.

32. Nashville *Banner*, September 2, 1964.
33. *New York Times*, September 3, 1964.
34. *Ibid.*

A Note on Sources

To a considerable extent, I have assembled this account from a montage of letters, reminiscences, newspapers, and government documents. No significant collection of Alvin York papers exists, but the files of several prominent Americans contain bits and pieces of the York story. The Hoover, Roosevelt, Truman, Eisenhower, and Kennedy presidential libraries all have letters pertaining to York, as do the collected papers of such diverse individuals as Cordell Hull, John J. Pershing, Frank Owsley, and Westbrook Pegler. Holdings in the Tennessee State Library and Archives were helpful in a number of ways. The records of several Tennessee governors include York correspondence, and the TSLA also has a small collection of scrapbooks and letters donated by the York family. The archives of the Tennessee State Board of Education shed considerable light on York's career in education. The Nashville *Banner* greatly facilitated my newspaper research by making available its clippings on York. The paper's files also contain an unpublished interview with York done in the 1930s. A variety of government documents proved especially helpful in my research. Most important was the Thomas File in the records of the Army War College at the National Archives. Among other items, the file contains "The Origin of War Legends," an account of the Argonne firefight from the German perspective. Unit records of the Eighty-second Division in the National Archives provided useful details about the division's involvement in the fighting of October 1918. This material is nicely supplemented by the *Official History of 82nd Division, American Expeditionary Forces* (Indianapolis: Bobbs-Merrill, 1920), compiled by the division officers. The Federal Archives and Records Center at East Point, Georgia, has York's draft card and the docket of the Fentress County draft board.

Any study of York's life must deal with a substantial body of journalistic and semi-autobiographical literature, most of which appeared between 1919 and 1930. George Pattullo, "The Second Elder Gives Battle," *Saturday Evening Post* (April 26, 1919), set the contours of the York legend as it took shape in the public mind. Samuel Cowan, *Sergeant York and His People* (New York and London: Funk and Wagnalls, 1922; Grosset and Dunlap, n.d.), offers colorful and sentimental vignettes of mountain life but little analysis of York or the culture which produced him. The two books prepared by Thomas Skeyhill, *Sergeant York: His Own Life Story and War Diary* (Garden City, N.Y.: Doubleday, Doran, and Company, 1928) and *Sergeant York: Last of the Long Hunters* (Philadelphia, Chicago, and Toronto: John C. Winston Company, 1930), grew out of a close collaboration between Skeyhill and York and therefore are especially valuable, but like the Cowan book they provide no rigorous scrutiny of their subject. Chapter 6 discusses these sources in considerable detail.

While virtually no academic writing about York himself exists, a number of books and articles have valuable information on various aspects of York's life and career. Books by Albert R. Hogue, *Davy Crockett and Others in Fentress County Who Have Given the County a Prominent Place in History* (Jamestown, n.d.) and *History of Fentress County, Tennessee, The Old Home of Mark Twain's Ancestors* (Nashville: Williams Printing Company, 1916), and William Lynwood Montell, *Don't Go Up Kettle Creek: Verbal Legacy of the Upper Cumberland* (Knoxville: University of Tennesse Press, 1983), give details about life in the Fentress County area. H.K. Carroll, *American Church History: The Religious Forces of the United States* (New York: Christian Literature Company, 1893) and Elmer T. Clark, *The Small Sects in America* (rev. ed., New York and Nashville: Abingdon-Cokesbury Press, 1949), discuss the origins of the Church of Christ in Christian Union. Edward Coffman, *The War to End All Wars: The American Military Experience in World War I* (New York: Oxford University Press, (New York: Macmillan, 1968); David Kennedy, *Over Here: The First World War and American Society* (New York and Oxford: Oxford University Press, 1980); and Laurence Stallings, *The Doughboys: The Story of the AEF, 1917-1918* (New York, Evanston, and London, Harper and Row, 1963) offer considerable insight regarding World War I and American life. My understanding of Appalachian society draws heavily on John C. Campbell, *The Southern Highlander and His Homeland* (New York: Russell Sage Foundation, 1921); Thomas R. Ford, ed., *The Southern Appalachian Region: A Survey* (Lexington: University of Kentucky

Press, 1962); Henry Shapiro, *Appalachia on Our Mind: The Southern Mountains and Mountaineers in the American Consciousness, 1870-1920* (Chapel Hill: University of North Carolina Press, 1977); and J.W. Williamson, ed., *An Appalachian Symposium: Essays Written in Honor of Cratis D. Williams* (Boone, N.C.: Appalachian Consortium Press, 1977). I obtained material about the film *Sergeant York* from several sources, including *Variety*; Gary Cooper, as told to George Scullin, "Well It Was This Way," *Saturday Evening Post* (February-April 1956); and Jesse Lasky, with Don Weldon, *I Blow My Own Horn* (Garden City, N.Y. Doubleday and Company, 1957). Charles Bohner, *Robert Penn Warren* (New York: Twayne, 1964) and Daniel Joseph Singal, *The War Within: From Victorian to Modernist Thought in the South, 1919-1945* (Chapel Hill, N.C.: University of North Carolina Press, 1982), directed my attention to characters modeled on York in the fiction of Robert Penn Warren. Finally, two articles, Robert Bellah, "Civil Religion in America," *Daedalus* (96, no. 1, Winter 1967), and John William Ward, "The Meaning of Lindbergh's Flight," *American Quarterly* (10, Spring 1958), provided much of my framework for interpreting York and his place in American life.

Index

Academy Award, 113
Adams, Harry J., 65
Aire River, 30
America First, 109, 111
American Legion, 45, 82, 125, 129, 132
Appalachia, 15-16, 51, 55-57, 63, 100, 104, 114
Apremont Woods, 33
Ardennes Mountains, 27
Argonne Forest, 23; fighting in, 27-39, 48, 58, 65, 115
Astor Theater, 110
At Heaven's Gate, 130
atomic bomb, 125

Baker, Newton, 50, 60, 66
Barnes, Howard, 111
Beaty, Tinker Dave 2, 17
Bellah, Robert, 57
Belleau Wood, 53
Boone, Daniel, 76
Bradley, Omar N., 119-120
Brady, William, 74
Brennan, Walter, 106, 112
Brier, Henry Clay, 88-90
Brooks, William, 3
Browning, Gordon, 90, 127
Bruen, E. J., 74
Burke, Henry, 90
Burnham, William P., 22, 29
Bushing, Arthur S., xi-xii, 77, 80
Bushing, Arthur S., Jr., 87
Buxton, George Edward, 19, 21, 40, 54, 141 n.39

Cagney, Jimmy, 105
Caldwell and Company, 83
Caldwell, Rogers, 83
Campbell, Marvin, 73-74
Camp Claiborne, Louisiana, 119
Camp Gordon, Georgia, 18
Camp Upton, New York, 21
The Cave, 131-32
Chamberlain, Neville, 109
Champocher Ridge, 33
Chandlee, Harry, 108
Châtel-Chéhéry, 30, 31, 32, 40
Chattanooga, Tennessee, 51-52, 60-61
Chicago Tribune, 74
Church of Christ in Christian Union, 10-12, 16-17, 98
Cincinnatus, 65
Civilian Conservation Corps, 120
civil religion, 57-58
Civil War, 2, 10, 16-17, 57
Clemens, John, 2
Clemens, Samuel, 2, 76
Clement, Frank, 134
Colditz, Max, 78
Colmar Pocket, 121
Committee on Public Information, 50
conscientious objectors, 21
Coolidge, Calvin, 89
Cooper, Gary, 105-07, 110-13
Cooper, Prentice, 90, 103
Cowan, Samuel, 93-99
Creel, George, 50
Crockett, Davy, 2, 76

Croix de Guerre, 39
Crowther, Bosley, 111
Cumberland Mountains, 1, 93, 129
Cutting, William B., 141 n.39

Danforth, Edward, 19, 21, 23, 31, 40, 44, 45, 47
Davis, Bette, 106
Davis, C.W., 90
Dayton, Tennessee, 98
Decauville Railroad, 30, 31, 38, 43, 46
Delk, Everett, 6-7
Distinguished Service Cross, 39, 45, 53
Duncan, George, 29, 43, 45, 47
du Pont, S. Halleck, 130

Early, Bernard, 33, 34, 44-45, 140 n.15
Eighty-second Airborne Association, 127
Eighty-second Division. *See* United States Army
Eisenhower, Dwight D., 129
Ellington, Buford, 132
Evins, Joe, 129-30

Famous Players-Lasky, 101
Fentress County, Tennessee, 1, 51, 64; description of, 4, 12; and World War I, 14; roads, 74-75; education, 75; people, 76-77, 78, 80-81; politics, 82-84, 85, 87, 89, 93-94, 97, 102, 107, 116-17. *See also* Jamestown, Tennessee; Pall Mall, Tennessee
Fentress County Gazette, 4, 14
Fentress County Selective Service Board, 17, 117, 128
Ferguson, Champ, 2, 17
Ferguson, Otis, 111
Finkel, Abem, 108
Flack, J.V.B., 16
Foch, Ferdinand, 27, 39
folklore, 2, 3, 37
Fonda, Henry, 105

Forrester, Robert L., 89
Fort Oglethorpe, Georgia, 60
Foster, Edgar M., 64, 71, 73, 74
Fourteen Points, 49
Frogge, O.O., 78-81, 84
Funk and Wagnalls, 93

Garrett, W.A., 80
gas, 26, 31
George Peabody College for Teachers, 87
German Army units: 2nd Württemberg Landwehr Division, 31-38, 45-46; 45th Reserve Division, 31-32, 45-46; 120th Landwehr Infantry Regiment, 31, 33, 37-38; 122nd Landwehr Infantry Regiment, 31; 125th Landwehr Infantry Regiment, 31; 210th Reserve Infantry Regiment, 33, 34, 37, 46; 212th Reserve Infantry Regiment, 32; 7th Bavarian Sapper Company, 33, 37
Gettysburg Address, 58
Giselher Stellung, 28
Glass, Lieutenant, 38, 41, 42, 43
Glenn, John, 132-33
Goldwyn, Sam, 106
Gore, Albert, 120
The Grapes of Wrath, 99
Great Depression, 86-87
Grosset and Dunlap, 94
Guthrie, William, 107
Guthrie, Kentucky, 130

Hale, John, 103
Harned, Perry L., 84-85
Hatch Act, 120
Hawks, Howard, 105-06, 108, 113
Help Sergeant York Committee, 130
Henderson, Thomas, 85
Hermitage Hotel, 103
heroes and heroism, ix-xii, 49, 54-57, 65-68, 72, 92-100, 103-04, 114-15, 121-24, 130-33, 134-36

Hill 223, 30, 31, 34, 44, 46
Hindenberg Line, 28
Hitler, Adolph, 101, 108-10
Hodgenville, Kentucky, 77
Hogue, Albert R., 2, 90
holiness movement, 11
Hollywood, 103, 106, 107, 112
Hooker and Hooker, 129
Hoover, Herbert, 109
Hoover, J. Edgar, 50
Hopkins, Raleigh, 84
Horton, Henry, 83-86
Huff, Preston, 3
Hughes, Howard, 105
Hull, Cordell, 58-60, 76, 87, 110
Huston, John, 108

industrial revolution, 49, 55
Internal Revenue Service, 128-30
Iowa, 108

Jackson, Andrew, 62, 65
James, Frank and Jesse, x, 7
Jamestown, Tennessee, 4, 18, 61,
    75, 78, 88, 127
Jamestown Light Company, 80
Japan, 101, 125
Jefferson, Thomas, 49
Johnson, Lyndon, 134
Johnson, W.M., 78

Kennedy, John F., 132
Khrushchev, Nikita, 132
Koch, Howard, 108
Korean War, 125
Korgia, Hercules, 65
Kuebler, Lieutenant, 42, 43

Land of the Pharoahs, 113
Lasky, Jesse, 101-08, 110, 113
Lea, Luke, 81-85, 86, 130
Lend-Lease, 111
Leslie, Joan, 106, 112
Life, 111, 127
Lilienthal, David, 118
Lincoln, Abraham, 58, 76-77
Lindbergh, Charles, 66-68, 109
Linder, James, 78

Lindsay, Julian R., 29
The Little Foxes, 106
Lorimer, George, 53
Lost Battalion, 29, 30, 52, 72. See
    also United States Army units,
    77th Division

McAdoo, William, 76
McAlister, Hill, 83, 84, 88
MacArthur, Douglas, 118, 119
machine gun, 49-50, 66
MacNamara, Robert S., 132
McKellar, Kenneth, 64, 87, 110,
    111
Marshall, George C., 53
Maryville College, 12
Massey, Raymond, 105
Medal of Honor, 30, 39, 45, 53,
    121, 122
Meet John Doe, 99
Metro-Goldwyn-Mayer, 106
Methodists, 10, 16
Meuse River, 24, 28
Mexican War, 5
Mr. Deeds Goes to Town, 99
Montenegro, 39
Montsec, France, 24
Morelock, Sterling, 65
Murphy, Audie, 121-24

Nashville, Tennessee, 2, 61-62, 93,
    103, 112
Nashville Banner, 59, 61, 64, 71,
    74, 83-84, 121, 126
Nashville Tennessean, 77, 82, 104,
    112, 128
National Guard, 132
National Youth Administration,
    89-90
New Concord, Ohio, 133
New Orleans, battle of, 65
New Republic, 111
New York City, 53, 58-60, 109-10
New York Herald, 62
New York Herald Tribune, 111, 122
New York Stock Exchange, 60, 74
New York Times, 45, 82, 111, 122,
    125, 134, 136

New York World, 74
Nineteenth Amendment, 62
Nolan, Dennis E., 54
North Korea, 125
Nye, Gerald P., 111

"The Origin of War Legends: An
    Investigation of the Alleged
    Feat of Sergeant York, October
    8, 1918," 27, 36, 40-44
The Outlaw, 105
Owsley, Frank, 130

Pall Mall, Tennessee, 4, 12, 19,
    56, 59, 62, 74, 78, 93-94, 107,
    126, 130, 134. *See also* Fentress
    County; Jamestown, Tennessee
Palmer, A. Mitchell, 50, 67
Paramount Pictures, 101, 106
Paris, France, 23, 25, 51-52
Parsons, Harry M., 31, 33, 140
    n.15
Parsons, Louella, 105
Pattullo, George, xii, 53-56, 58, 66,
    92
Payne, Bruce, 87-88
Pearl Harbor, 100, 116
Peay, Austin, 78-83
perfectionism, 11
Pershing, John J., 25, 28-29, 52-53,
    66
Pickford-Lasky Corporation, 101
Pile, Conrad, 1-2, 93
Pile, Mary, 1
Pile, Rosier, 12, 17, 19-20, 47, 61,
    62, 64, 106, 112, 116
Pont-à-Mousson, 25-26
Pope, Lewis, 83-84
Prohibition Party, 120

Rayburn, Sam, 119, 129-30
Red Cross, 117
Red Scare, 50, 67
Reichsarchiv, 40-42
Rickenbacker, Eddie, 25
Ridgway, Matthew, 119-20, 134
Roberts, Albert H., 61-62, 76
Rockefeller, John D., 50

Roosevelt, Eleanor, 119
Roosevelt, Franklin D., 87, 108-10,
    111
Roosevelt, Theodore, x, 65
Rotary Club, 60, 64, 71-74
Russell, H.H., 9
Russell, Jane, 106
Ryman Auditorium, 62

St. Mihiel salient, battle of, 24-28,
    30
San Juan Hill, battle of, 65
Sarris, Andrew, 113
Saturday Evening Post, xii, 53, 92,
    122
Savage, Murray, 47
Scopes Trial, 98
Sedan, France, 27-28
Sergeant York, 92, 95, 99-116, 120,
    128, 135
Shapiro, Henry, 55, 57
Sharp, W.N., 74
Skeyhill, Thomas, xi-xii, 40,
    94-100, 123
Smith, L. D., 86
Stahlman, E.B., 61, 64, 83-84
Stalin, Joseph, 125
Stallings, Laurence, 22
Standard Oil, 126
Stephens, Paul, 89-90
Stewart, Lieutenant, 33
Stewart, Thomas, 87
Stockton, George, 77, 81, 86
Swindler, Henry, 39-40

Tennessee Board of Education,
    78-80, 84-85, 88-91
Tennessee Central Railroad, 61
Tennessee General Assembly,
    77-79, 129
Tennessee Society, 58-59
Tennessee Supreme Court, 86
Thoma, Lieutenant, 37, 43
Tobacco Road, 112
To Hell and Back, 122, 124
Tracy, Spencer, 105
Truman, Harry S., 118, 125-26,
    129

Tumulty, Joe, 60
Twain, Mark. See Clemens, Samuel
Twentieth Century Fox, 101

United States Army units: 26th Division, 24; 28th Division, 44; 77th Division, 29, 30, 72; 82nd Division, 19, 22-26, 28-48, 70, 119-20; 328th Infantry Regiment, 19, 26, 43-44, 46; 164th Infantry Brigade, 29; 2nd Battalion, 30-48; Company G, 19, 26, 31-48; 114th Field Artillery Regiment, 81; 157th Field Artillery Regiment, 30. See also Lost Battalion.
United States Army War College, 39-40, 45
United States House of Representatives, 60, 120
United States Senate, 81
University of Harriman, 12
Upper Cumberland Times, 126

Varennes, France, 28, 30
Variety, 110-11
Verdun, France, 24, 28
Vietnam, 113
Vollmer, First Lieutenant, 33, 34, 36-37, 41, 43, 46

Wallace, Henry A., 119
Wallis, Hal, 105
Warner, Harry, 105
Warner Brothers, 99, 105-08
Warren, Robert Penn, 49, 130-32
Washington, George, 49, 58, 65
Washington, D.C., 53, 58-60, 110
Watson, Edwin, 87
Wecter, Dixon, 49
Wesley, John, 11
West Point, 22, 29
Wetherill, Richard, 43
Wheeler, Burton K., 109
Wheeler, J.T., 78
White, Walter, 83
Whittlesey, Charles, 29-30, 52, 72

Williams, Frank Asbury, 9, 107
Wilson, Woodrow, 49, 51, 60, 67, 82
Wolf Gang, 3
Woodfill, Samuel, 52, 66, 72
Works Progress Administration, 89
World War I, 4; begins, 14-16; and American society, 49-50; and civil religion, 58; and modern war, 66-68; York's attitude toward, 100-101, 109
World War II, 94, 116-24
Wright, H.N., 85
Wright, William L., 59, 64, 71, 76, 78, 80, 86
Wycherly, Margaret, 106

York, Alvin C.: writings about, xi-xii, 40, 92, 94-99; youth of, 4-9; and weapons, 5, 7-8, 18, 23-24, 34-36, 107, 140 n.19; and religion, 9-13, 15, 17-21, 47-48, 51, 58, 70, 98-99, 103, 112-13; and faith and violence, 12-13, 20-22, 26, 47-48, 54-55, 98-99, 125; and marriage, 15, 61-62, 150 n.31; and financial problems, 15, 71-74, 87, 97, 128-30; reluctance to serve, 16-22; diary of, 22-23, 94-95; and first combat, 24-26; and firefight, 30-48, 76; and criticism from American soldiers, 44-45; and John Pershing, 52-54; and Saturday Evening Post, 53-56, 58; and Appalachia, 55-57, 63, 76-77, 93-100, 104, 114; and civil religion, 57-58; sources of popularity, 65-68; and Charles Lindbergh, 66-68; and problems of being a hero, 69, 71-74, 96, 130-32; and readjustment to home life, 69-71, 91; and founding of York Agricultural Institute, 75-85; and political connections, 81-85; as president

York, Alvin C. *(continued)*:
  of York Agricultural Institute,
  85-89; generosity of, 86-87, 90;
  and *Sergeant York,* 99-115; and
  Bible school, 102-03, 113, 126,
  128; and World War II, 116-24;
  and political ambitions, 120-21,
  126; and Audie Murphy,
  121-24; and oil business, 126;
  and declining health, 127-34;
  and John Glenn, 132-33; and
  children, 150 n.31
York, George Edward Buxton, 127,
  134
York, Gracie Williams, 8-9, 15, 61,
  86, 95, 106, 112-14, 128-30,
  133-34
York, Jim, 89
York, Mary Brooks, 4-8, 19, 59,
  61-62, 87
York, Uriah, 3, 5
York, William, 4-6
York Agricultural Institute, 77-81,
  85, 97-98, 102, 108
York Highway (U.S. 127), 6, 75,
  98, 134
York Industrial School, 79
York Museum, 94
Young Men's Christian Association, 51